This Poor Man Called
STORIES AND SONGS OF DAVID
VOLUME 1

What a great idea! This is a special book born of passion for the power of the biblical stories about David and the preaching of the Psalms that arose from the stories. The telling of the stories is done in a creative and yet realistic way, drawing from the author's awareness of the historical context and scholarly issues—all of this with surprising imaginative twists along the way. The exposition of the related Psalms is clear and filled with compelling applications to the lives of people everywhere in all times.

RICHARD E. AVERBECK
Professor of Old Testament and Semitic Languages
Trinity Evangelical Divinity School

David Barker has invited us into the power of story through the life and psalms of David. With exegetical skill and practical application, he immerses us into the world of Israel's shepherd-king, whose voice echoes living truths about the character and nature of God, and what we can learn about ourselves in the process. You will be not only spiritually rewarded by this read, but richly blessed as well.

JON KORKIDAKIS
Adjunct professor, Heritage College & Seminary, Cambridge, ON
Author of *Touching God* and *The Trojan Horse of Leadership*

David Barker has been a beloved Old Testament professor for four decades and has also been busy pastoring in local churches. He has wonderfully bridged the gulf between academia and the assembly. His students have gained insight from his particular interest in the Psalms. I recently heard David preach from an imprecatory psalm in a local church. He didn't hold back from Psalm 10's message with shepherding words about "times of lament" and a blunt and stern warning to all tyrants of the world. I will not soon forget his message; it offered me a glimpse into David's prophetic heart.

The following exploration of several Davidic psalms in both exposition and story allows the author to offer a glimpse into his shepherd's heart. His stories nourish the soul and model the shepherd's heart of another David we all know.

STEVEN JONES
President, The Fellowship of Evangelical Baptist Churches in Canada

This book is gold for those who sense they are stuck in a rut with how they traditionally study and interpret Scripture. Even for those who don't sense it, they probably are. Taking the psalm titles seriously and matching David's poetic longings with episodes in his life, Barker deftly retells the biblical stories with added historical and cultural details, helping modern readers understand the accounts closer to the way original hearers would have. Then he shows how the matching psalms take on fresh meaning and clearer application. It's a hermeneutical *tour de force*.

D. BRENT SANDY
Manuscript Curator and Researcher, Grace College and Seminary
Formerly professor at several colleges & universities, most recently Wheaton College

Having known Dave Barker as a very close friend now for over three decades and having heard him speak on many occasions on his beloved Psalms, I am thrilled to see this two-volume work reaching many who have not had either the privilege of his friendship or that of hearing him. His love for Scripture, his careful exegesis of the Old Testament and his passion for God and his truth—key hallmarks of Dave's life—are abundantly evident here. May God use these pages powerfully for the glory of his Name and the good of his people.

MICHAEL AZAD A.G. HAYKIN
Professor of Church History, Heritage Theological Seminary, Cambridge, ON
& Professor of Church History, The Southern Baptist Theological Seminary, Louisville, KY

Three decades ago, I learned to love the Psalms in Dr. Barker's classrooms. The lessons learned then prepared me for the twists and turns of life and ministry through the intervening years. As I read these stories and expositions, I became David's student again. I commend this book to those who need to learn more about God's faithfulness and how to call out for it.

TIM BAHULA
ABWE Canada missionary

STORIES AND SONGS OF DAVID

VOLUME 1

DAVID G. BARKER

Heritage Seminary Press, Cambridge, Ontario
An imprint of H&E Publishing, Peterborough, Ontario, Canada

hesedandemet.com

© 2022 Heritage College & Seminary. All rights reserved. This book may not be reproduced, in whole or in part, without written permission from the publishers.

Scripture taken from the Holy Bible, New International Version®, NIV®. Copyright © 1973, 1978, 1984, 2011 by Biblica, Inc.™ Used by permission of Zondervan. All rights reserved worldwide. www.zondervan.com

The "NIV" and "New International Version" are trademarks registered in the United States Patent and Trademark Offices by Biblica, Inc.™

Cover and book design by Janice Van Eck

This Poor Man Called: Stories and Songs of David
Volume 1
David G. Barker

Paperback ISBN 978-1-77484-063-4
Ebook ISBN 978-1-77484-064-1

To Lorraine,
a true *'ezer kenegdo* in all the fullness
of what that phrase means.

And further,
to my esteemed colleague and friend,
Dr. Stanley K. Fowler.

At the time of writing and publishing these essays he has been silenced in both voice and written word by a debilitating stroke. The loss to the church and world is immeasurable.

This latest chapter of his life story has prompted songs and prayers of deep lament, along with songs and prayers of trust and hope in our loving God, everything the stories and songs under study here embrace.

CONTENTS

VOLUME 1

Foreword	ix
Acknowledgements	xiii
Introduction	1

PROLOGUE
The unnoticed noticed: The story that begins it all — 17
1 Samuel 16:1–13

CHAPTER 1
A fortress in the face of snarling dogs — 27
1 Samuel 16:14–19:17; Psalm 59

CHAPTER 2
Gratitude when things go bizarre — 45
1 Samuel 21:10–15; Psalm 34

CHAPTER 3
Confidence in the face of betrayal — 63
1 Samuel 21:1–9; 22:6–13; Psalm 52

CHAPTER 4
God is my help — 81
1 Samuel 23:1–29; Psalm 54

Selected bibliography — 99

FOREWORD

I met Dave Barker in the mid-70s at Grace Theological Seminary in Indiana. It didn't take long for us to realize we were kindred spirits. We enjoyed studying the Old Testament indepth, with the goal of someday teaching its wonders to Christ's church and those training to be pastors. Following seminary, Dave and I went our separate ways. Dave has faithfully served the Lord at Heritage for over four decades. I just completed my fourth decade of service at Dallas Theological Seminary. Dave and I have enjoyed catching up when we meet at the annual conference of the Evangelical Theological Society. It was special for me to serve as the external dissertation examiner for Dave's son Joel, as he was completing his doctoral studies at McMaster Divinity College.

A few summers ago, Dave and I reunited at Elim Lodge Christian Resort and Conference Centre in Buckhorn, Ontario, through our mutual friend David Rivers, who was serving as director at Elim. When he discovered Dave and I had been seminary classmates, he invited us to team teach a series on King David. (Lots of "Davids" were involved in this!) Each day during the week-long conference, I focused on events from the life of David recorded in 1 and 2 Samuel, while Dave did expositions of Davidic psalms that originated in those events. It worked well, and I'm delighted

xi

our joint venture served as the impetus for this book and its forthcoming companion volume.

During that week at Elim, I was impressed not only with Dave's expositional gifts, but also his pastor's heart. In addition to our teaching sessions, we both wanted to minister in other ways to folks who were visiting Elim that week. The Lord gave us that opportunity. A young man who had recently trusted Jesus as his Saviour was seeking to find his way as he embarked on his journey of faith. Dave and I spent time with him, offering counsel and prayer. I saw Dave's pastoral heart that week, both inside and outside the pulpit.

I see that same pastoral heart shining in this book. Dave is concerned that readers ask themselves three questions when they study Scripture:

1. What do we learn about God?
2. What do we learn about ourselves as the people of God?
3. What do we learn about the world?

These are fundamental questions we should always ask as we read the Bible. In this book, you will find a reliable guide to answering those questions.

Dave's strategy in this book is brilliant and superbly executed. He retells the biblical story in an engaging manner that will transport you back into the event so that you can see, hear, smell and feel what is happening. The style is creative, yet solidly rooted in the biblical text, so that its authoritative principles emerge. Dave's approach resonates with me. Every Wednesday night my grandsons, ages six and four, stay overnight with my wife Deb and me. Before bed I tell them a Bible story, frequently taken from the accounts of David and his mighty men. I use the same techniques Dave employs, and watch with delight as they experience the wonder of God's work in history as if they are there in that long ago time and place. Why shouldn't we adults experience that same kind of wonder as we engage the biblical stories? Dave helps us do that. The value of the approach is it helps the lesson stick, so we can more readily become doers, not just hearers, of the written Word.

Dave's expositions of the accompanying psalms display his expertise as an interpreter, not to mention his great love for these inspired prayers and the God to whom they are addressed. He has a God-given ability to make the meaning of the text clear and relevant. As Dave helps me connect to David's prayer, I come away from these expositions knowing what God expects from me and motivated to obey his will.

Thanks, Dave, for writing this book. I'm sure the Lord will use it to help God's people grow in their love for his written Word and in their commitment to serve the Son of David, the *living* Word.

Robert B. Chisholm, Jr.
Chair and Senior Professor of Old Testament Studies
Dallas Theological Seminary, Texas
January 25, 2022

ACKNOWLEDGEMENTS

A work like this cannot come into being without the help of numerous people. Many thanks to Marianne Vanderboom who has been studying the Psalms with me for a number of years now and continues that pursuit in her doctoral work. Thank you Marianne for your edits and comments. Thanks to Joel Barker for his edits, comments and getting the Hebrew into appropriate form. Thanks to Rick Reed for reading and commenting.

I am grateful for the opportunities to preach the Psalms in a number of churches and try out the idea of combining story and song in sermon form. Special thanks to Ed Fontaine who allowed me to do a summer series in his church using some of the chapters in the book as sermons.

Thank you to David Rivers for inviting me to come as a speaker several times to Elim Lodge Christian Resort and Conference Centre, as well as to John Friesen who also had me come and speak at Muskoka Bible Centre on several occasions. These were places where I honed my expositions of a number of psalms.

Special thanks to Robert Chisholm for writing the Foreword. Thank you, Bob, for your kind words. It was very special to spend time with you at Elim. Your storytelling about David sparked this whole project.

I wish to thank Heritage College & Seminary which has allowed me to teach the Book of Psalms for over twenty years now. The Psalter has become the heartbeat of my personal and communal spirituality. As I teach the book year after year, the voices of the psalms become even more deeply embedded in my life. I trust the same is true for the students who pass through my classroom.

A special thank you goes to Michael Haykin who has relentlessly encouraged me to continue with this project and gave me the opportunity to publish with the newly formed Heritage Seminary Press, an imprint of H&E Publishing.

Thank you to Janice Van Eck and the staff at H&E Publishing who actually got this work into a publishable form.

Finally, I am deeply grateful to my wife Lorraine, whose love and support over almost five decades of marriage has made it possible to meet the demands of both a pastoral ministry and an academic career.

INTRODUCTION

Genesis of this project
Stories and songs of David the Israelite king, the sweet singer of Israel.

The genesis of this project began in the summer of 2016 when David Rivers, then Director of Elim Lodge Christian Resort and Conference Centre near Peterborough, Ontario, found out that two of his friends, Dr. Robert Chisholm, chair of the Old Testament department at Dallas Theological Seminary, and myself, were classmates in seminary way back in the seventies. So, he invited both of us to partner for a week of speaking at Elim. Without really knowing what the other was doing, Bob spoke in the morning on a story about David from 1 and 2 Samuel, and I did series on selected psalms in the evening. From that I mused on an idea of putting stories and psalms together rooted in the psalm title that attributed the psalm to David and which also noted a historical event in David's life. The project would include an expository and somewhat imaginative rewrite of the biblical story and an exposition of the psalm in light of the realities of the story.

I tested the idea at a seniors retreat in 2017 at Muskoka Bible Centre near Huntsville, Ontario, in which I read the story in the morning sessions and did an exposition of the psalm in the evening sessions. I was encouraged by that very patient and affirming group to keep the project moving forward.

Then, in the summer of 2018, I was invited by Dr. Ed Fontaine to do a series at Springvale Baptist Church in Stouffville, Ontario, using a few of these stories and psalms. Following the tradition of Canada's storyteller Stuart McLean, of the CBC series *The Vinyl Cafe*, I sat on a stool and read my expositional remake of the story cited in the title of the psalm. Then I moved to a podium and did a more formal exposition of the psalm, ending with points of application and implication from both the story and the psalm.[1]

The result is this collection of nine stories and psalms/songs of David.[2] We've decided to publish them in two small volumes, the first with this introduction and a prologue containing the opening story of David being anointed as king, followed by the first four stories and songs. The second volume includes five more stories and songs, ending with Psalm 18, paralleled in 2 Samuel 22, as an epilogue. The essays follow the chronological history of David's life through 1 and 2 Samuel and 1 Chronicles. The second volume also includes an Appendix containing an essay on imprecations in the Psalms that I have published elsewhere,[3] and has been reprinted with permission for this project.

The goals of this collection include: (1) to hear the stories of David in a living storytelling fashion;[4] (2) to reacquaint readers with the place and value of storytelling as a means to communicate

---

[1] I don't pretend to write and speak at the level of Stuart McLean. I was reminded of that by one listener who, with a smile, commented, "That was good, but you are no Stuart McLean."

[2] There are fourteen psalms that have a reference to David's life. However, several of them refer to the same event in different psalms (eg. Pss 57 and 142), and two titles refer to events that are not recorded in Scripture (Pss 7, 30). In my count there are nine distinct stories in the biblical record and so nine essays in this study.

[3] David G. Barker, "The Church and Imprecations in the Psalms: The Place of the Call to Curse in the Life of the Church Today," in *Ecclesia Semper Reformanda Est—The Church is Always Reforming: A Festschrift on Ecclesiology in Honour of Stanley K. Fowler*, eds. David G. Barker, Michael A.G. Haykin, Barry H. Howson (Kitchener: Joshua Press, 2016), 65–87.

[4] I am convinced that doing a storytelling "sermon" on a biblical narrative text is a form of biblical exposition. The expositor works hard at understanding the theological point(s) of the story and seeks to bring those out in the retelling of the biblical text. This is the same thing an expositor does in doing any expositional sermon on a text whether in the Epistles, Gospels, Prophets and more.

truth about God, ourselves as the people of God and the world; (3) to provide a popular but serious exposition of selected psalms; (4) to engage the titles in the psalms; and (5) to bring these psalms to life by recounting the stories that prompted or came to serve as backdrops for these psalms. Along the way, my hope is there will be a renewed delight in the reading of these stories and psalms, as well as perhaps a modelling of doing creative expositional storytelling alongside preaching and teaching from the Psalms.

Story

A well-known rabbinic saying states, "God made people because he loves stories." Who doesn't like a good story well told? As children, having someone read a story to us, even when we knew the story already, was a highlight of the day. As adults, so often in a sermon in which the preacher is working hard at a careful exposition of the text, it is when the preacher inserts a story or illustration that our interest is piqued and we reengage with the sermon.

The power of story is captured in the Canadian icon Stuart McLean, Canada's storyteller. Week after week on Sunday afternoons he told stories about a fictional couple named Dave and Morley along with their children, Stephanie and Sam, their dog Arthur, and a variety friends and neighbours on the CBC program *The Vinyl Cafe*. My colleague, Marianne Vanderboom, wrote an insightful blog that captures the heart and beauty of McLean's stories. But she also points us to the place story has in the sacred Scriptures and in our lives. I reproduce her blog here in full:

> *Tell Me a Story*
> For the last seven years, I have driven to the barn pretty much every Saturday morning between 9:00–10:00 in the morning, and for the last seven years, as often as I could, I listened to as much as I could of Stuart McLean's *The Vinyl Cafe*. I am late to *The Vinyl Cafe*; apparently, it has been running for two decades. 1 have grinned and laughed and thought and even shed tears with Dave and Morley and the gang. I have lingered in the car to ensure I heard the end of the stories, and when I heard the words, "l'm Stuart McLean; so long for now," I would turn off the ignition, sigh, wipe tears, laugh again and get out of the car.

This past Saturday, I missed Stuart. I was just a bit too late leaving the house, and all I heard was the final song of his story-and-song show. That made me especially sad because this past Saturday was Stuart McLean's last show. He's leaving *The Vinyl Cafe* in order to fight cancer—melanoma. The airwaves next Saturday will be lonely without that slightly raspy voice that always sounds like it's smiling. I will miss his stories.[5]

I have often marvelled at the genius that is Stuart McLean. He tells simple stories—stories about ordinary folk, absurd folk—in a simple way. He read his manuscripts straight up, no extemporaneous speaking, no stand-up comedy, just a well-written story read well, and people flocked to listen. I wonder sometimes if we have a bit of a snobbish attitude toward stories. We adults listen to propositions, lectures, sermons, speeches and TED Talks, but stories? Stories are for children. And yet . . . here was a guy who read stories in halls around the country, and people bought tickets to hear him, and they tuned in to listen to him on the air. Nothing high-tech. No computer-generated imagery, no special effects, no 3-D, immersive, large-screen glitz. Just a voice. A quiet, wry, raspy voice. And we listened and laughed and cried and thought and laughed and cried some more. Dave and Morley became friends. We cried when their dog died. We laughed when Dave got himself into his endless scrapes; he was so much like all of us. We were glad when the two of them, even when it was really tough to do so, made choices for love and loyalty and kindness and decency and courage and neighbourliness. Just a story, but it made our lives richer.

That's the beauty of story. It disarms the hearer. It draws him in and gets him invested and then it turns and prods and convicts.

God knew that. I think that's why so much of Scripture is written as a story. "In the beginning, God created the heaven and the earth," and we immediately recognize the opening lines of a story. Oh sure, there are laws and psalms and letters and sermons, but underlying all of them is a story. Think of

---

[5] Stuart McLean passed away on February 15, 2017.

how many psalms are embedded in story, just as an example. Because while we are taught by law and psalm and letter and sermon, we connect most deeply, I think, with story.

Jesus knew that. I think that's why he told so many parables. Oh sure, he gave instructions and teachings, but so many times he answered with a story. The story has a way of getting in behind defenses and presuppositions and forces us to look at things through new eyes. Instructions and teachings are important, but they engage the head. Sometimes it is the heart that must be turned, and the heart is most easily turned, I think, by story.

But we are a society that has lost our story. There was a time, not so many years ago, that most people shared a story. The fancy word is "metanarrative." Most people knew and believed the biblical master-story, at least at some level. That is no longer the case. As a society, we no longer know the story. And, I think, even as a church, we have lost our sense of story. We have relegated the story to Sunday School, considering the story to be "milk" from which we must grow up so that we can eat the "meat" of theology (or something), forgetting that the story is also theology. We no longer trust story.

But the really awful kicker is that we no longer trust proposition either. Information and misinformation are so easily obtained. "Fake news" has become a thing. Pictures lie all the time. We live in a "post-truth" society that is suspicious of all proposition, lecture, sermon, speech and TED Talk. We don't know what or whom to trust anymore.

I wonder if the two are connected. Perhaps when we cast off story as something childish and silly, something from which we grow up, our theology loses its moorings and is cast adrift into "post-truth." I wonder if, in our quest for solid proposition and sound theology, we have forgotten the power of a good story well told. Of course, the solid proposition and sound theology are important, but so is the story.

Stuart McLean knew the power of story. For twenty years he wrote and read stories to adults. People didn't come to his shows to hear propositions about Dave and Morley. They came to hear stories.

Perhaps we should take a page out of his book. Perhaps we should return to the story. Perhaps we should tell more stories. Perhaps we should remember that the story is theology, too.

> Tell me the old, old story of unseen things above,
> Of Jesus and His glory, of Jesus and his love.[6]

Sidney Greidanus noted correctly that "of all the biblical genres of literature, narrative may be described as the central, foundational, all-encompassing genre of the Bible."[7] Almost forty percent of the Bible is narrative. When we read or hear a story we share the experience and enter into the story, listening and watching with tension and anticipation of how it is all going to turn out. Is Jephthah really going to keep his vow and sacrifice his daughter? Is Micaiah really going to confront the king and tell him bad news when 400 other prophets have told him to go to battle and succeed? How is Hannah going to deal with her adversary, her clueless husband and then the miraculous gift of a son? We enter the stories, and in all our study of the Bible it is usually the stories we remember best.

Song

Along with storytelling, songs and music have been a core part of cultures and society from the beginning of time. How often when people have gathered to share stories and life, perhaps around a campfire, someone has brought along a guitar and amidst the conversation and laughter we sing and hear music? It has been like that since time immemorial.

It is interesting that the New Testament does not give a lot of instruction on how to conduct a worship service or a gathering of the local church. We are told we need to hear the Word of God preached and taught (2 Tim 4:2), we need to hear the public reading of Scripture (1 Tim 4:13) and that prayer is an important component (Eph 6:18); beyond that, not a lot, except for one more—*singing*. Twice in the Epistles, the apostle Paul instructs the

---

[6] Reprinted here with permission. Marianne Vanderboom, "Tell Me a Story," December 31, 2016; www.glimpsesoftheking.ca.

[7] Sidney Greidanus, *The Modern Preacher and the Ancient Text: Interpreting and Preaching Biblical Literature* (Grand Rapids: Eerdmans, 1988), 188.

church to sing "psalms, hymns and spiritual songs" (Eph 5:19; Col 3:16).

Music was considered to be crucial in the worship life of the church. There are several reasons for this. First, music and song allow serious theological truth to be put into a memorable form as poetry that can be remembered and sung. We cannot but think of the beautiful poetic doxology celebrating the marvelous transcendence and incomprehensibility of God in Romans 11:33–36. Or we might think of the powerful lyrical description of the submission, servanthood and sacrifice of our Saviour Jesus Christ in Philippians 2:6–11. Both of these may well be the lyrics to songs sung in the first century church.

Second, music and song allow the breadth of life—its pain and its blessing—to be articulated in a way that is artistic and meaningful. We cannot go far in either the psalms or in popular contemporary music without singing about loss, disappointment, joy and hope. Third, it brings people together and gives them a common voice of joy, lament, protest, trust and adoration of God. Whether in church or a U2[8] concert people sing as one common people the lyrics they have come to know so well. And fourth, it engages the aesthetic. It brings richness and beauty into the life of the singers and hearers of music as reflections of the image of God who is a God of beauty and creativity.

While the references to psalms by Paul to the Ephesian and Colossian churches may not be limited to the Book of Psalms, it is certainly inclusive of that book. As such, while the music of the first-century church was broader than just the psalms (hymns and spiritual songs), the Book of Psalms was in many ways the hymnbook of the first-century church. There are a number of good reasons for this. First, the psalms articulate a theology of God that is almost incomparable to anything else in the Bible. We hear the soaring expressions of God's covenantal love, his holiness, his mercy and grace, his desire for redemption, rescue and salvation, his invitation to lament in his presence, his willingness to hear imprecations of one's enemies, his acceptance of confession and willingness to forgive and his justice for the poor, orphan and widow. We hear of the power and beauty of the sacred Scriptures,

---

8 U2 is an Irish rock band.

of the stories of God's workings in history, the hope of a messianic king, the beauty of the place of God's residence and the presence of God himself in the community of God's people, both in their personal lives and in the journeys of the nation.

Second, the Book of Psalms uniquely gives voice to the people of God in addressing God. Bernhard W. Anderson prefaces his book with the following:

> It is reported that Athanasius, an outstanding Christian leader of the fourth century, declared that the Psalms have a unique place in the Bible because most of Scripture speaks *to* us, while the Psalms speak *for* us (see the *Service Book*, p. 45; United Church of Canada, 1969). There is much truth in this observation. Much of the Bible, in the conviction of the community of faith, is the medium of God speaking: "the word of God in human words," to cite a familiar expression. But the psalms of the Old Testament are different. Here, for the most part, we find people addressing God in response to God's overture, in the moods and modes of lament in times of distress, of thanksgiving in times of liberation, and in hymnic praise in times of rejoicing in the goodness and wonder of God's creation and providence. In this sense, the Psalms may speak "for" us, by expressing the whole gamut of response to God's grace and judgment and thereby teaching us how to pray.[9]

Much of the Bible is God speaking to us through the Law or through the prophets and apostles. Some of it is sagacious elders speaking to young adults in the wisdom books. However, the psalms are different. They are the pray-ers' and singers' voices ascending upward to God. Yes, they are the revelation of God to us. They are "God-breathed" and divine revelation. But they are unique in that they are the heartfelt expressions of the children of God to God. Nothing is masked. While the apostles and prophets preached and wrote on what and how the children of God *ought* to believe and act, the psalms serve as examples of what and how the

---

9 Bernhard W. Anderson with Stephen Bishop, *Out of the Depths: The Psalms Speak for Us Today*, 3rd ed., revised and expanded (Philadelphia: Westminster John Knox, 2000), ix. Emphasis in original.

Introduction

children of God actually *did* believe and act. That's why Martin Luther declared that "the Psalter is the favourite book of all the saints." He commented further:

> [Each person], in whatever his circumstances may be, finds psalms and words which are appropriate to the circumstances in which he finds himself and meet his needs as adequately as if they were composed exclusively for his sake, and in such a way that he himself could not improve on them nor would find or desire any better psalms or word.[10]

Third, the psalms give us the full range of responses to life with its joys and celebrations, as well as its pain and losses. We have psalms of praise and doxology that call upon the people of God to sing hallelujah (Ps 113). We have psalms of thanksgiving that open with the call, "Give thanks to the LORD for he is good" (Ps 107:1). Then we have psalms of trust that give us confidence in our God as our shepherd (Ps 23), and rock and fortress (Ps 18). At the literary centre of the Psalter we have a collection of seven psalms celebrating the LORD as King (Pss 93–99), the foundational theological idea of God in the Psalter. We have songs of Zion celebrating the Old Testament residence of God (Ps 87) that can be brought into the church as the present dwelling of God the Holy Spirit (1 Cor 3:16–17). A collection of fifteen psalms celebrate the pilgrimage of faith from a village to the sanctuary (Pss 120–134), and they now become the voice of all Christian pilgrims in their journey from earth to the heavenly Jerusalem (cf. Heb 12:22). Several psalms celebrate the importance of the sacred Scriptures (Pss 1, 19, 119), and we hear wisdom in the psalms (Ps 73). Finally, as a surprise to most of us, the single largest category of psalms is none of the above, including praise, thanksgiving or trust. Rather, the single largest category of psalms is *lament*—psalms that bring the pain and brokenness of life into the worship of the temple, synagogue and church (Pss 13; 22; 44:17–26). This includes lament for sin, in what we call penitential psalms (Ps 51). This latter point is

---

[10] Cited from Artur Weiser, *The Psalms: A Commentary* (Philadelphia: Westminster John Knox Press, 1962), 20.

important for the study of our selected psalms, since they all revolve around David's life and—inevitably—the pain and trouble he faced. We will see several genres of psalms in our study, but lament will be the dominate tenor of these psalms.

It's important to note that while we can place the psalms into discreet categories, there is often a mixture of feelings in the individual psalm. Praise, trust and lament can be found in a single psalm. So while one of these categories may be the dominant voice heard in the psalm and may be further evidenced by the compositional structure of the psalm,[11] we need to be always looking for the full gamut of response to life and its vicissitudes. We will see that mixture in the psalms selected for this study.

Further, the various categories of psalms are not placed in discreet groups throughout the book. A psalm of praise stands next to a psalm of lament. A cry for help in one psalm bleeds into "O give thanks for the LORD for he is good" in the next. "Darkness is my closest friend" ends Psalm 88 which is immediately followed by "I will sing of the LORD's great love forever" as the first line of Psalm 89. Eugene Peterson writes:

> Experience arrives randomly. Jack-grief and Jill-pain tumble over one another down the same hillside. Doubt and faith are in a wrestling match, first one on top and then other, in shifting supremacies. We cannot order our lives into discreet categories; life comes, in Hopkins's adjectives, "dapple, fickle, freckled."[12]

This kind of dialectical symphony of psalms is what gives them authenticity and immediacy in the life of God's people, and allows this voice of worship to engage all the realities of life, including the painful ones we are so often encouraged to "get over," or leave at the door of the church. J. Todd Billings writes:

> Rather than being one-dimensional, our affections need to become agile and multidimensional through being reshaped

---

[11] Lament, praise and thanksgiving psalms each have distinct compositional structures.
[12] Eugene Peterson, *Answering God: The Psalms as Tools for Prayer* (New York: HarperCollins, 1989), 107.

by God through the Psalms. Let us grieve and protest and trust and praise together before the Lord. The Psalms give us a way to pray in many keys, major and minor, while directing us to the source of true hope: the Lord and his promises.[13]

Psalm titles

The exposition of each of the nine psalms is based in the psalm title that heads the psalm. One hundred and sixteen of the 150 psalms in our English Bibles have a title or superscription of some kind.[14] Seventy-three of them are ascribed to David. The titles reflect a number of different things such as authorship, the name of a collection, the type of psalm, musical notations, use of the psalm in an event or liturgy, as well as historical notes in the life of David. The titles are usually integrated into verse 1 of the psalm, but some of the longer ones are actually verse 1 in the Hebrew text (and sometimes verses 1 and 2).[15]

Some have questioned the authenticity and reliability of the titles. However, recent studies have affirmed their reliability and that they need to be recognized as giving us helpful information in reading the psalms in which they occur. The ascription "of David" or "by David" is a translation of the preposition *le*[16] and David's name (and the same for "of/by Asaph/Solomon/Moses" etc.). The preposition *le* can be translated "of," "by," "to," "for," or "concerning," and does not necessarily mean authorship. In a number of cases, the preposition *le* is attached to the Hebrew word for "the director of music" and would best be translated "to" or "for" since it seems that the psalm was written for that person's use.

However, an authoritative Hebrew grammar known as GKC[17] states that a *le* attached to a name commonly denotes authorship.

---

13 J. Todd Billings, *Rejoicing in Lament: Wrestling with Incurable Cancer & Life in Christ* (Grand Rapids: Brazos, 2015), 40.
14 English versions of the Old Testament are translated from the Hebrew Bible. The Septuagint, the Greek translation of the Old Testament, has titles for all the psalms except Psalms 1 and 2.
15 English versions of the Old Testament separate out the title and so some of the psalms in our English Bibles have different verse numbering than the Hebrew Bible. This study will stay with the English Bible versifications.
16 For the Hebrew purists, I am using SBL's General Purpose Style for transliterations.
17 *Gesenius' Hebrew Grammar*, ed. Emil Kautzsch, trans. Arthur E. Cowley, 2nd ed. (Oxford: Clarendon, 1910), 129c.

This is strengthened by the fact that the New Testament seems to affirm this in citations of the psalms ascribed to David (Mark 12:36; Acts 1:6; 2:25; Rom 4:6; 11:9). That David would be the author of these psalms corresponds well with what the Bible says about David. He was called "the hero of Israel's songs" (2 Sam 23:1),[18] was a skilled player of the lyre (1 Sam 16:16–23) and was well-known as a songwriter (2 Sam 1:17–27; 22:1–23:7). The post-exilic chronicler records that David had a significant role in shaping and developing Israel's worship life at the sanctuary (1 Chron 16:4–7, 37–42; 23:2–6; 25:1–7). So, it appears that we are on solid ground in seeing David as the author of the psalms that are ascribed to him. This collection of stories and songs aligns with that conclusion.

There is also significant discussion of the historicity or veracity of the historical references that refer to David. Fourteen psalms refer to an incident in David's life, and twelve of them are found in 1 and 2 Samuel and 1 Chronicles.[19] It is uncertain as to whether David himself wrote these historical notices or whether they came from a later scribe who connected the psalm with an event in David's life. There is every reason to argue that David may well have written the notices and that the event described in the title led to his writing of the psalm. But there is also good reason to think that a later scribe could have inserted these notices based on an accepted tradition by the Israelite community of the David story behind the psalm. These notices set in writing the background event for the community of readers in the temple and synagogue, and come into the New Testament and to us today as the authoritative setting for reading these psalms. Bruce Waltke writes:

> Against the prevalent skepticism of academics regarding the originality, and so the veracity, of the psalms' superscripts, both the universal tradition of Davidic authorship and the empirical evidence support the notion that $l^e d\bar{a}w\bar{i}d$ means "by David," and that David authored the psalms attributed to

---

[18] Sometimes this phrase is translated "the sweet singer of Israel," or "Israel's beloved singer" (cf. NIV, 1984, 450).
[19] Psalms 7 and 30 have no reference to David's life in the biblical text.

him, and that the historical notices that associate fourteen psalms with his career are credible.[20]

Hence, in this study we affirm the Davidic authorship of the psalms under study. It will also read the historical references in the titles as authoritative for understanding the situation standing behind the psalm. It is interesting to note that the content of several psalms seems to conflict with their titles (eg. Pss 34, 60). However, this simply raises the reality of our lack of knowledge of how the psalm came about in that particular historical circumstance. This means we need to take seriously that the title and psalm have come to us together, and recognize that psalms often reflect conflicting emotions and responses to how life is happening. These are the things that have given the psalms their living and dynamic impact on the lives of God's people for millennia.

The form of the books

As noted, these two volumes are a selection of nine psalms, all ascribed to David, following in chronological order the historical reference in the title to the event in David's life recorded in 1 and 2 Samuel and 1 Chronicles. I retell the story in my own words often using the voice of another character in the story (eg. one of David's men in the cave when David had the chance to kill Saul). I have worked hard at getting at the theological and prophetic centre of the story as recorded in the Samuels and 1 Chronicles, but I have brought a creative twist to the retold story. A basic understanding of biblical stories is that God is the Hero (capital H) of every story. However, the human protagonist or hero (lower-case h) is the featured character in the story, and the actions of such heroes are always measured by their reactions and responses to the Hero of the story. This is the basis for "theologizing" the stories rather than simply "moralizing" them, something we don't need a God-breathed Bible to do.

The story then leads into a verse-by-verse exposition of the psalm. There are some introductory notes and then a statement of the point or message of the psalm. The exposition of the psalm

---

[20] Bruce K. Waltke, James M. Houston and Erika Moore, *The Psalms as Christian Worship: A Historical Commentary* (Grand Rapids: Eerdmans, 2010), 92.

follows an expository outline grounded in the stated point and seeks to stay deeply embedded in the actual text of the psalm. The expositions follow the English of the 2011 edition of the New International Version,[21] but are rooted in a close reading of the Hebrew text.

At the end of each story and song essay, I conclude with asking three questions: What do we learn about God? What do we learn about ourselves as the people of God? and What do we learn about the world? I believe the Bible is asking these three basic questions in seeking to shape a theocentric and biblical worldview. There are multiple questions and answers that emerge from these three that the Bible explores, but these serve as the basis for making any further applications or developing implications.[22]

Moving forward

In concert with the goals stated at the beginning of this Introduction, here are some of things we will find in this study. First, we will find a theology of God as sovereign and King. He is the Hero of every story, and every prophetic narrative is founded upon a theocentric worldview with God reigning as King. In the Psalms, yes, he is pictured as shepherd (Ps 23), warrior (Ps 46:8–9) and judge (Ps 96:13), but these were all functions of an ancient Near Eastern king, the cultural setting for understanding God's kingship in Israel.[23] Further, Psalm 103:19 affirms, "The Lord has established his throne in heaven and his kingdom rules over all." Even in lament, the psalmist cries, "Listen to my cry for help, my King and my God" (Ps 5:2). David, the psalmist, affirms in Psalm 22, "Dominion belongs to the Lord, and he rules over the nations" (v. 28).

Second, we will find that all of life is lived in the presence of God. The prophetic narrator is careful to tell every story in concert with the approval or disapproval of God. Sometimes it is

---

[21] The Holy Bible, New International Version (Grand Rapids: Zondervan, 2011).
[22] Darrell W. Johnson in his book, *The Glory of Preaching: Participating in God's Transformation of the World* (Downers Grove: IVP Academic, 2009), 59–75, 158–171, provides a helpful distinction between application and implication, and pushes us toward developing the implication/worldview of the text more than specific applications which are so varied from person to person and church to church.
[23] This is well-articulated by Robert B. Chisholm, Jr., "A Theology of the Psalms," *A Biblical Theology of the Old Testament*, ed. Roy B. Zuck (Chicago: Moody, 1991), 257–301.

subtle and has to be thought through carefully as to which response of God is in play. Other times it is explicit and we find words like "favour" (eg. Samuel in 1 Sam 2:26) or "rejected" (eg. Saul in 1 Sam 15:26). We read these narratives with the God of the morality, ethics and spirituality that we know from elsewhere as the lead character in the story. The psalmist writes:

> These things I remember
> as I pour out my soul:
> how I used to go to the house of God
> under the protection of the Mighty One
> with shouts of joy and praise
> among the festive throng (Ps 42:4).

Whether lament, praise, thanksgiving or trust, the psalms are the King's word on our responses to him in worship and prayer out of our varied experiences and life-stories.

Third, we learn that life and the life of worship are an interactive dynamic of despair and hope, failure and success, sin and forgiveness (with consequences). David's sin with Bathsheba finds forgiveness in an abject confession (Ps 51), but with consequences of sorrow and death. We find that prayer and worship are more of a dynamic life-reality and less a formality. The first two psalms in the Psalter serve as flanking pillars at the entrance to the "throne of grace." Psalm 1 prepares us for blessedness and focuses our lives on meditation on holy Scripture and the choices of moral and ethical righteousness over the path of wickedness. Psalm 2 guides our worship, and we see God as King, mocking those who dare challenge his rule as we hear the call of the cantor, "Kiss his son, or he will be angry and your way will lead to destruction" (v. 12). These two flanking pillars set the ethos and govern the spirit. With this kind of heart, we approach boldly, regularly and vigorously into the full gamut of emotions, feelings and intellectual and theological inquiry.

So, how to do we learn to use these songs and stories in guiding our pilgrimages of faith and hope? First, read the stories, and read them *as* stories. We need to read seeing the beginning, middle and end of the story. We need to see the comic or tragic plot of the stories.[24] We need to read them not so much looking for historical data points or geographical locations, as important as they are. Rather, we need to learn to read looking for the answers to the key questions of God, ourselves and the world, and the God-centred worldview that emerges from these questions. This is how we read theologically, and how we read looking for both application and implication. I would encourage readers to read the biblical narrative and associated psalm before reading my "take" on the story. This will ground the reader in the biblical text and help the reader understand why I have taken the story in the direction I have chosen.

Then, what about the psalms? We learn to speak them in the way children learn to speak with their parents. We speak what we read and hear. Yes, we can refine our understanding by learning the categories and structures of psalms, but we first learn the freedom of responding to our heavenly King in the midst of our story with the full breadth of feeling and emotion. When we do this, we will find we are praying and worshipping the God and King of our salvation revealed in Jesus Christ more than we know, and our lives will be truly God/Christ-centred and life-filled.

---

[24] An excellent introduction on reading stories well is William W. Klein, Craig L. Blomberg and Robert L. Hubbard, *Introduction to Biblical Interpretation*, 3rd ed. (Grand Rapids: Zondervan, 2017), 420–437.

PROLOGUE

THE UNNOTICED NOTICED: THE STORY THAT BEGINS IT ALL

BIBLE READING
1 Samuel 16:1–13

Story ♦ 1 Samuel 16:1–13

As Jesse stood up from tying what seemed to be his one-thousandth sheaf, he saw him. Down the road there was coming a lone man, snowy white hair, flowing beard, leading a calf. In an instant Jesse knew who this man was. *What was the famous, fierce and dangerous prophet Samuel doing coming to his village, Bethlehem? What had happened? What had they done wrong, or right?*

Jesse turned and walked briskly to the village. The other elders had already gathered. The news had spread quickly—Samuel is coming, and he is leading a calf. The silence was ominous as the prophet walked through the village to the central square. He sat on a bench beside the well. Hesitantly, carefully, the elders, as a group, approached. Yaakov, the head elder spoke.

"*Shalom, nabi Shemuel.*"

Samuel returned the greeting, "*Shalom 'alekah.*"

And then from Yaakov, "Do you come in peace?"

"*Shalom*. Yes, in peace, I have come," Samuel replied.

"*Lizboah layhweh ba'thi*—I have come to offer a sacrifice to the LORD," the prophet went on. "Prepare yourselves for the ceremony."

Quickly the group dispersed to return to their homes to perform the preparatory rituals. A service of worship to God! The prophet Samuel here personally! This was huge!

As Jesse turned to go, Samuel called quietly, "Jesse, come here."

"Yes, master," Jesse replied.

"I am coming with you to your house," Samuel said.

"Yes, master," Jesse replied again. *What is this all about?*

As the two walked together Samuel said,

"Gather your sons. I am here for another purpose."

"Yes, master", Jesse replied. "Ah, why are you *really* here?"

Samuel responded, "I am here to choose a new king for Judah. The sacrifice is a camouflage in case Saul hears about it. God told me to do it this way."

Jesse was dumbfounded. *What is going on?* He knew that their present king, Saul son of Kish, was not doing well. He had heard that Samuel was pretty annoyed at him. *But, a new king? And from one of his sons? O God, what are you doing?*

When Jesse and his family had gathered at the house, Samuel performed a little ceremony of consecration. But only Jesse knew the real purpose of all this. Back to the village centre they went. An altar had been built and the fire was burning, and the sacrificial calf stood quietly tied to a tree. In front of the villagers, elders and family of Jesse, Samuel quickly and deftly slaughtered the calf, skinned it and laid the carcass on the flames. The blood was carefully poured and sprinkled on and around the altar. The smell of burning flesh and smoke filled the air.

Then Samuel gave Jesse the nod. Jesse quickly whispered to his oldest son, Eliab, "Go stand in front of Samuel." Somewhat confused, Eliab stood in front of the frightening prophet. Eliab was tall, handsome, strong—a born leader. The firstborn child. *This one's a lock*, Jesse thought. Samuel looked him over. But then he slowly shook his head, and then turned to Jesse, "No, not this one. Please bring another son."

For the second time Jesse was dumbfounded. *What do you mean not the one? He is first. He is the head son!* In a daze, Jesse touched the arm of Abinadab his second son. He took his turn in front of

Samuel. Again, the seeming sense of satisfaction. But then the shake of the head. Rejection number two.

"Jesse, another son please." This time it was Shammah who stood before Samuel. Another rejection. For all seven sons the conclusion was the same. All good, solid, healthy, intelligent men. All rejected.

Jesse was mortified. *What was Samuel after?* Samuel was speaking to him. He seemed confused. "Jesse, do you have any more sons?" Jesse replied, "Well, master, yes, I do. I have a *qaton*—a little one, their baby brother. He's out in the pasture looking after the sheep." *Surely not David*, Jesse thought. *He's just a kid. This is not the way we work. We're after a king here. We need the biggest, the best, the one with charisma. That had been their choice in King Saul. Oh sure, he had gotten off the rails with God, but this is what the other nations around them all had. How could they hold their own with the Philistines and Canaanites without this kind of king? David? A child? The little one?*

The prophet's voice penetrated his reverie, "Go get him. We will not sit down until he comes." Jesse called over to a young boy and whispered, "Go find David. You stay and look after the sheep." The boy ran off. They waited. Finally David came and stood before Samuel. Yes, a youth, but good looking and strong.

This time, instead of another rejection Samuel heard the LORD say, "Rise and anoint him; this is the one." He put his hand on David's shoulder and the boy sank to his knees. From the folds of his cloak, Samuel took out a ram's horn of olive oil. In front of the wide-eyed circle of people gathered, including a father, a mother, elders and seven rejected brothers, he poured the oil over David's head and shoulders. The next king in Israel had just been anointed.

Everyone was thunderstruck. So that's what this was—a coronation, an anointing as king! Eliab and the others, all rejected. Further, King Saul, our choice, rejected. And now this—David, anointed as king!

Samuel picked up his things to leave. Jesse touched his arm and pulled him aside. "What just happened here? Why David? Why not Eliab, Abinadab, Shammah or the others?" Samuel said, "This is what God said to me, 'Do not consider his appearance or his height, for I have rejected him [Saul]. The LORD does not look at the things people look at. People look at the outward appearance, but the LORD looks at the heart.'"

And with that Samuel disappeared back up the road by which he had come.

Reflections and lessons

1. What do we learn about God?

(a) We learn *God loves to choose the marginalized,* the "little guy," the *qaton*. David was the little one in the back pasture looking after sheep when Jesse's seven sons are brought to the ceremony of worship. We are reminded of the apostle Paul's words,

> Brothers and sisters, think of what you were when you were called. Not many of you were wise by human standards; not many were influential; not many were of noble birth. But God chose the foolish things of the world to shame the wise; God chose the weak things of the world to shame the strong. God chose the lowly things of this world and the despised things—and the things that are not—to nullify the things that are, so that no one may boast before him (1 Cor 1:26–29).

(b) We also learn *God will reject the powerful when they take on their own power.* Power in and of itself is not evil or contrary to God's kingdom. But power used for one's own aggrandizement, self-sufficiency and abuse of others is completely antithetical to God's means of rule and will be judged and rejected. One only needs to think of the powerful people inside and outside the church who used power to dominate and abuse others, and the brutal consequences for both the victim and the perpetrator.

The central point of the story is the pivotal statement by God, "The LORD does not look at the things people look at. People look at the outward appearance, but the LORD looks at the heart" (1 Sam 16:7). Our hearts are bare before God. David, later in his moral failure, wrote, "My sacrifice, O God, is a broken spirit; a broken and contrite heart you, O God, will not despise" (Ps 51:17). When we start with God, we start with the heart.

(c) *God often breaks the patterns of normal thinking.* While cultural and Torah norms were usually followed by Israel, sometimes we see "breakouts" that indicate the redemptive perspective of God that often rose above prevailing culture. The Torah norm was for the eldest son to have the ruling place in the family. He was considered to be the family priest and had birthright privileges. That is why Jesse was so confounded in the choice of David. Elsewhere in biblical stories Jacob was chosen over Esau, Abel over Cain (although there were "heart/faith" issues in Cain's sacrifice). The norm also was that men led in both family and society. But Deborah (and Jael) was empowered over Barak (Jud 4:1–24), and even in the New Testament, Priscilla seems to have taken a lead role over her husband Aquila since she is mentioned first when the two are named (Acts 18:18–26; 2 Tim 4:19; cf. 1 Cor 16:19 where Aquila is mentioned first). The norm is that the strong lead the weak. However, Ehud, a man "weak in his right hand" (i.e., left-handed, Judg 3:15) was chosen by God to deliver his people from the Moabites. Gideon, who declared, "My clan is the weakest in Manasseh, and I am the least in my family" (Judg 6:15) and whose lack of faith was demonstrated by a fleece (Judg 6:36–40), led a miniscule army in a night-time rout of the Midianite army (Judg 7:8–25). Jephthah, rejected by his brothers because his mother was a prostitute, led his family and tribe to victory against the Ammonites (Judg 10:6–11:40). Further, he is listed in the New Testament "Hall of Faith" chapter in spite of the child-sacrifice of his daughter (cf. Heb 11:32). Samson, a failed and flawed Nazirite, as a tragic hero, in his dying act delivered Israel from the Philistines (Judg 13:1–16:31) and is also listed in Hebrews 11.

While we learn about the people God uses, it speaks powerfully to the nature of the God we serve and worship.

2. What do we learn about ourselves as the people of God?

Two questions emerge from this story in what we learn about the people of God. First, what does God look for in his people in doing his mission and work in the world? Second, what kind of people do we need to be and look for as we serve God and each other in his kingdom?

We are so often vulnerable to the externals. We are flooded with the models, the books and seminars, the stories of success, growth and prosperity. We are impressed by appearance, presence and a resume. We celebrate superior skill or talent, education—MDiv., PhD., DMin., a sense of presence and power, clothes with designer labels, natural beauty or handsomeness, physical strength or wholeness of health, a flashy and engaging personality.

Saul was the people's choice. He was a head taller than any other man in the nation. They wanted "a king like the other nations" that would lead them into battle, a king in whom they could place their political and military trust. It was a disaster. Samuel was forever trying to salvage God and truth from this man's rule.

This is a foundational reflection for any follower of Christ, but particularly for leaders. In choosing our leaders we can usually judge *competence*. Sometimes *chemistry* is a little harder to know ahead of time if the leader under consideration is not well known. But the critical factor in choosing a leader is *character*. This takes work to ascertain. It means wide referencing, thorough questioning and broad consultation. Further, this speaks to the necessity of ongoing accountability of the leader even when the position supersedes everyone else. Independence and autonomy are deadly realities for any leader, but especially in the church of Jesus Christ. We learn that we need to be very careful in what we look for and what we expect from our leaders. This does not give excuse for incompetence when we are expected to be competent. It does not give excuse for lack of preparation when we are expected to be prepared. It does not mean we don't look for talent or gifting. We all serve the body of Christ with the God-given gifts and talents we can bring. But the work of God is spiritual ministry empowered by God's Spirit through prayer and a heart for God.

Our hearts are what God sees. As a result, the father's instruction to his son, "Above all else, guard your heart, for everything you do flows from it" (Prov 4:23) becomes a crucial teaching for anyone who names the name of Christ. This is taken to a deeper level when we read the life of David who is known as a man after God's own heart (1 Sam 13:14; Acts 13:22). The description of David in contrast to Saul is spoken by Samuel when he announced to Saul he had been rejected as king (1 Sam 13:11–14).

So, we hear the message, "Guard your heart," but we also hear the message, "Seek God's heart." We do both of these by engaging the spiritual disciplines of reading and reflecting on Scripture both privately and communally, a healthy, diverse and intimate prayer life, serious commitment to, and active participation in, Christian community (local church), keeping sabbath (in function and principle, not law or form) and other disciplines such as fasting, journaling and times of silence and solitude.

Reflecting on the events of this story, Asaph, the chief musician appointed by David, wrote the following of his king:

> He chose David his servant
> and took him from the sheep pens;
> from tending the sheep he brought him
> to be the shepherd of his people Jacob,
> of Israel his inheritance.
> And David shepherded them with *integrity of heart*;
> with skillful hands he led them (Ps 78:70–72, emphasis mine).

While David was anything but perfect (we'll see several instances of his imperfection in the following pages), that foundational notion of a heart turned toward God, a heart in tune with God's heart, is stamped firmly on the character of David as seen by the biblical storytellers and poets.

We also learn from this story that we can have great confidence in who we are and what we have to offer in the service of God. David, a *qaton*, a term specifically used to describe something small, or extra or not needed, is the one chosen by God to lead the nation. Further, he was the eighth son. Seven was a number signaling completeness or totality. The narrator clearly and deliberately makes the point that David was number eight, perhaps an "oops," as we might say it today. We all have a place and role in the mission of the kingdom of God. Yes, we are all different, but we are all part of the enterprise. The apostle Paul in 1 Corinthians 12 talks about the church as a body, and that all parts of the body are needed for a body to function well. Further, he emphasizes that its parts should have "equal concern for each other." So, no matter who we are, what giftings we have been given, what place we have in the church of Christ, and perhaps in some sense a *qaton*, we can have great confidence in who we are (our identity as found in Christ) and what we have to offer in the service of Christ and his church. This is how God does things. This is the Jesus way. All too often we fall back to what seems to work, to what makes sense to us, to what we are used to in the business and corporate domains of our lives. We are almost afraid to trust the Holy Spirit and afraid to believe the Jesus way is truly different.

It also tempers our expectations of each other. We are all very ordinary people. We are special to God but ordinary to each other. We're all in Christ's kingdom because of grace, God's infinite grace. Let's face it, who uses weak and flawed people like Ehud, Gideon, Jephthah and Samson? Yet, each one of these people, in the mix and mess of how God works, brought deliverance to the nation. Churches are made up of very ordinary people. Our leaders are very ordinary people. When the church embraces the strategies for success in the corporate world, it becomes something other than God's gathered people called the church. Zechariah said it long ago, "'Not by might nor by power, but by my Spirit,' says the LORD Almighty" (Zech 4:6).

3. What do we learn about the world?

The world is the "other nations" who look for a king. The world looks for power, position and presence in its leaders. Success and wealth are the gods of the world. When Israel asked for a king "such as all the other nations have," they had fallen into the values of a world that stands in antithesis to God's kingdom and rule. Samuel was appropriately distressed and went to the LORD with his concern. The answer from God was clear, "They have rejected me as their king" (1 Sam 8:7). Samuel did all he could to warn them of the destructive and oppressive path they were choosing, but they refused to listen. "No!" they said. "We want a king over us. Then we will be like all the other nations, with a king to lead us and to go out before us and fight our battles" (1 Sam 8:19). The church is not exempt. Size, wealth, power and status have too often infiltrated the church as measures of success and value. Somehow we know this is not where God wants us to be.

The issue for Israel was not their desire for a king. That was part of the plan for Israel from the beginning (cf. Deut 17:14–20). But he was to be everything a king in the nations was not. But that was not sufficient for Israel. The values of power, position and wealth in their leader were too attractive for them. And so, Saul, son of Kish, became their king. It was a moral, ethical and national disaster. Hence, the story we have just recounted finds its place in the history of God's people—a story of the countermeasures to the people's choice and the norms of power allocation.

But the world can be even more dangerous than simply

standing in passive opposition. Samuel was concerned that if Saul found out what he was doing he would kill him. That is why the subtle act of deception is part of the story. Not only do we see in the story the action of God in bringing about *his* choice of king and confronting the people's choice, but we see that when God's people go down the path of the world they become active enemies of God's work and will in the world. Samuel, the prophet of God, feared for his life from Israel's king, while doing what God had instructed him to do. So now, the king of the nation is a real and active threat to the agent of God's voice and message to the nation. Some of the most powerful enemies of Christ's church and kingdom are those who were once part of it. As the church, we dare not diverge from the moral, ethical and spiritual values the Scriptures articulate for its leadership. Sometimes it is hard for the church to reject the cultural norms for leadership and to resist taking its direction from successful management and leadership strategies that do not embrace servanthood, sacrifice, suffering and even death (cf. Jesus, Phil 2:5–11). Sometimes it is hard not to bend in the direction of "like the other nations." However, that path will inevitably cost the church and the mission of God in the world dearly.

God loves to reverse the norms. A cross stands at the centre of the Christian faith. That cross, with its image of suffering, sacrifice, humility and death, dominates the biblical story. The story of David we have just read is one point in that story. In the foolishness, weakness and poverty of the cross, God brought redemption and forgiveness into the world. It goes against all the normal patterns we pursue, such as: power and strength are better than weakness, winning is better than losing, big is better than small, health is better than sickness, comfortable living is better than suffering and gain is better than sacrifice. The message that the church proclaims is that the message of the gospel is based in a complete reversal of the normal pattern of power and conquest. Again, listen to Paul speak to the Corinthians,

> For the message of the cross is foolishness to those who are perishing, but to those of us who are being saved it is the power of God. . . . For since in the wisdom of God . . . God was pleased through the foolishness of what was preached

[the cross] to save those who believe. The Jews demand signs and Greeks look for wisdom, but we preach Christ crucified: . . . Christ the power of God and the wisdom of God (1 Cor 1:18–24).

Final word

It is good news that God is a God who works through the ordinary, who in grace reversed the power structures and chose a cross and who knows our hearts. Why? Because it gives us all a chance! As we think about who and what we are as the people of God in the world, we see God's choice of the *qaton*, the ordinary, perhaps even the odd and left out. We see God's rejection of the self-sufficient, and the centrality of the spirit of the cross even in the contrast of David and Saul. Ultimately, we see the core requirement for God's blessing: a heart totally given to God.

CHAPTER 1

A FORTRESS IN THE FACE OF SNARLING DOGS

BIBLE READING
1 Samuel 16:14–19:17
Psalm 59

Story ◆ 1 Samuel 16:14–19:17

King Saul was on a mission—a mission of murder, and the songster and warrior, David, son of Jesse, was in his sights. David was the eighth and youngest of Jesse's sons, a shepherd-boy from Bethlehem. I am one of King Saul's soldiers. I saw David come into King Saul's court and soothe King Saul's tormented mind with his skilful hands on the harp. What a relief for all of us when he played! When King Saul went into one of his raging fits, it was intolerable for all of us. It was as if a demon had come and possessed him.

David became a favourite of all of us. Perhaps as King Saul's soldiers we could have become jealous of him, but he brought so much good and was such a winsome person it was impossible not to like him. He rose rapidly in the army ranks among us. He actually became King Saul's personal armour bearer.

A defining moment came in a battle with our arch-enemies, the Philistines, in the Valley of Elah. We were completely immobilized by one of their warriors, a gargantuan man by the name of Goliath. With the Philistine army camped on one side, ours on the other, day after day Goliath marched into the valley and mocked us, laughed at us, called for someone to do battle with him and defied our God. Our king, King Saul, a giant of a man himself, hid in his tent, much to our dismay and shame. Did he not believe that our God, who we know as Yahweh, was superior to their gods? Did he not trust in our God for victory? Where was his faith and courage?

Then David showed up. He had been on leave from King Saul working with his father in Bethlehem. He was bringing food for his brothers who were part of our army. We could hardly believe what happened next. First, he asked who the warrior in the valley was. Then he was taken to the tent of King Saul, and there, evidently, he tried on the king's armour, but it was far too big for him. He then came out of the tent and promptly went down into the valley where the Philistine was, armed only with a slingshot and a pouch. We watched him pick up some stones from the brook that ran through the valley. The boy and the giant approached each other. The Philistine laughed and mocked. Then with a shout of confidence in our God, David spun the sling around his head, the stone flew and down went the giant, struck squarely between the eyes. With a shout, we ran out of our camp and down into the valley. The chase was on—all the way to Gath and Ekron, two of the Philistine cities on the coast. Victory was ours!

While it may be hard to believe neither King Saul nor Abner our commander recognized who David was. But when the rout was over Abner reported to King Saul who David was, and he was given a high rank in the army. But things were starting to turn, and not in a good direction for David.

It started when David became really popular with the people. When King Saul and his army returned to Jerusalem after the great victory over the Philistines, the women in the towns and villages along the way came out to meet him dancing and singing. But the song they sang went like this:

> Saul has slain his thousands,
> And David his tens of thousands.

This galled King Saul. Jealousy and fear took over his heart. We all knew things were going to go badly for David, but there was nothing we could do.

On the very next day, King Saul had one of his fits again. He was acting like a man possessed. David was playing his harp trying to soothe his tormented mind. This time it was good that David was young and quick. King Saul took the spear that happened to be in his hand and hurled it at David. David dodged. The spear sunk itself into the wall behind David's head. Then, King Saul tried to have David killed in battle by putting him over a thousand men. But it didn't work. David led one successful campaign after another. Next, he tried marrying him off to his daughter Merab, with the intent that, as Saul's son-in-law, David would be obliged to lead even more battle campaigns—and hopefully get killed. But David refused the marriage stating he was from too humble a family to become the king's son-in-law.

But then along came Michal, another daughter of King Saul. She had fallen passionately in love with David, and King Saul saw his chance again. This time he sent some of his attendants to David to try and persuade him to marry Michal. But David's answer was the same, "Do you think it is a small matter to become the king's son-in-law? I'm only a poor man and little known." But this time King Saul had an answer. He told his attendants to tell David that he could earn the right to marry his daughter. All that he wanted was a bride-price that would involve the death of a hundred Philistines. He was sure David would be killed in that venture. Well, it didn't work out that way. David and his men went out and killed *two* hundred Philistines. So, Michal became his wife. He became even more popular with both the army and the people, and King Saul became even more afraid of this rising star.

Enter Jonathan, King Saul's son. We all knew he was heir to the throne and that if anyone should be threatened by David it would be him. However, for whatever reason, Jonathan and David became fast friends. He knew the throne was David's, not his. So he went to his father and persuaded him to stop trying to kill David. King Saul actually said, "As surely as the LORD lives, David will not be put to death." For a while, all was well. But another war with the Philistines broke out and David was again victorious. That was the last straw. Again, a spear buried itself in the wall behind David's head as he was playing for the king.

That night, I and a few others were sent by King Saul to David's house to kill him when he came out in the morning. It was the last thing we wanted to do, but we were under the command of our king. But both he and Michal outsmarted us. She knew what we were up to and so she let him down through a window and he got away. When he didn't come out in the morning, Michal told us he was ill. Now, it is completely dishonourable to kill a man in his bed, but when we reported all this to our king, he sent us back and told us to bring David to him while still in his bed so he could kill him himself. So, back to the house we went, crashed through the doors and into the bedroom. What did we find? We found a stuffed dummy looking like a man in bed, clearly Michal's doing. So now Michal is in trouble with her father. But when King Saul asked her why she had let his enemy get away she lied and said he had threatened to kill her if she didn't.

So now, the chase was on. For months, even years, David will be a fugitive. Our king, King Saul, and the rest of us will be in hot pursuit. But David's faith and loyalty to our God will sustain him. The musician who played so skilfully to soothe King Saul's possessed mind will write and sing songs that come out of these dark places of dodging spears, escaping through windows at night and hiding in caves and cliffs in the Judean wilderness. In this world of danger and desperation, he will become known as "the hero of Israel's songs" and will write music and poems that will become our voice in the worship of our God.

Song ♦ Psalm 59

For the director of music. To the tune of "Do Not Destroy." Of David. A miktam. *When Saul had sent men to watch David's house in order to kill him.*

1 Deliver me from my enemies, O God;
    be my fortress against those who are attacking me.
2 Deliver me from evildoers
    and save me from those who are after my blood.

3 See how they lie in wait for me!
    Fierce men conspire against me

for no offense or sin of mine, LORD.
4 I have done no wrong, yet they are ready to attack me.
   Arise to help me; look on my plight!
5 You, LORD God Almighty,
   you who are the God of Israel,
  rouse yourself to punish all the nations;
   show no mercy to wicked traitors.

6 They return at evening,
   snarling like dogs,
   and prowl about the city.
7 See what they spew from their mouths—
   the words from their lips are sharp as swords,
   and they think, "Who can hear us?"
8 But you laugh at them, LORD;
   you scoff at all those nations.

9 You are my strength, I watch for you;
   you, God, are my fortress,
10   my God on whom I can rely.

God will go before me
   and will let me gloat over those who slander me.
11 But do not kill them, Lord our shield,
   or my people will forget.
In your might uproot them
   and bring them down.
12 For the sins of their mouths,
   for the words of their lips,
   let them be caught in their pride.
For the curses and lies they utter,
13   consume them in your wrath,
   consume them till they are no more.
Then it will be known to the ends of the earth
   that God rules over Jacob.

14 They return at evening,
   snarling like dogs,
   and prowl about the city.

15 They wander about for food
and howl if not satisfied.
16 But I will sing of your strength,
in the morning I will sing of your love;
for you are my fortress,
my refuge in times of trouble.

17 You are my strength, I sing praise to you;
you, God, are my fortress,
my God on whom I can rely.

Introductory notes
Set in the context of Saul's death warrant for David noted in the title, in this psalm we find an intense appeal from David to God to rescue him from his vicious and bloodthirsty attackers—attackers he calls "snarling dogs" (cf. vv. 6, 14). In turn David affirms God is his fortress, his strength, his vindication and his trust, and so is worthy of praise.

While the story of the siege of David's house informs the content of the psalm, the psalm reaches far beyond that event. The reference to the nations in verse 5 indicates David had a broader view of his call of God to action and confidence in his response. However, it seems the psalm was composed with the siege as the first horizon of backdrop, and we can read the psalm with that story shaping the power and passion of the psalm.

1. It is a lament psalm.
Psalm 59 is the sixth of a string of eight lament psalms beginning in Psalm 54 and ending with Psalm 61. Lament psalms compose the largest category of psalms in the Book of Psalms.[1] There are more lament psalms than praise psalms, thanksgiving psalms, trust psalms or any other category of psalms. This speaks to the place of such a voice in the worship life of God's people. Life is hard, and the Scriptures give us a voice to come to our God boldly and openly to express our pain, frustration, despair and even

---

[1] For a helpful listing of categories see Appendix B in Bernhard W. Anderson with Stephen Bishop, *Out of the Depths: The Psalms Speak for Us Today*, 3rd ed., revised and expanded (Philadelphia: Westminster John Knox, 2000), 219–224.

anger. The Book of Psalms was the central voice of worship in the times of Old Testament Israel, into the synagogue in Jesus' day and into the first-century church. Twice the apostle Paul instructed the church to sing the psalms (Eph 5:19; Col 3:16). While this may not have been limited to the Book of Psalms, it certainly would not have been any less. The twenty-first-century church would do well to recover the voice of lament contained in the psalms in its worship.[2]

2. It is written to or for the director of music.
Evidently Psalm 59 was handed over to the director of music to teach the choirs who then taught the people the song. While all the psalms became the public voice of worship, this reference makes it explicit that the congregation was to sing it as part of their communal expressions. We don't know who that director of music was, but we do know David appointed a number of Levites to lead the people in worship. Asaph was appointed the chief, and Heman and Ethan (Jeduthun) were his direct associates (cf. 1 Chr 16:4–6, 41–42). There are psalms from all three of these worship leaders.

3. The title uses the phrase, "Do not destroy."
This is probably a reference to the tune or melody to which the psalm was sung. The NIV has the phrase, "to the tune of," but that is not in the biblical text. However, it is probably a correct interpretation of what the phrase means. It is the third of three psalms in a row that carry this note (Pss 57; 58; 59).

4. The psalm is "Of David."
As I indicated in the Introduction, there is some question as to what the phrase in Hebrew means. However, while the best way to render the phrase seems to be "Davidic," I am arguing that the psalm has its source in David as the composer.

5. It is a *miktam*.
The term *miktam* first occurs in Psalm 16, and then only in Psalms 56–60, all of which are attributed to David when he is in great

---

[2] There has been much written on this topic in the last fifteen years. A brief, pointed and practical work is Federico G. Villanueva, *It's OK Not To Be OK: Preaching the Lament Psalms* (Carlisle: Langham Preaching Resources, 2017).

danger. The meaning of the term is unknown, but it seems to be a musical notation.

Outline of the psalm
Psalm 52 has five parts with two refrains:

1. An opening plea (vv. 1–2)
2. An appeal to see and defend (vv. 3–5)
Refrain: snarling dogs (vv. 6–7)
3. An affirmation of confidence in God (vv. 8–10)
4. An appeal to expose (vv. 11–13)
Refrain: snarling dogs (vv. 14–15)
5. A final statement of confidence (vv. 16–17)

> ## Message of the psalm
> In Psalm 52 we discover that we can call on God with a deeply intense appeal to rescue us from our vicious and bloodthirsty attackers—attackers the psalmist calls "snarling dogs" (cf. vv. 6, 14). In turn, we affirm that God is our fortress, our strength, our vindication and our trust, and so is worthy of praise.

Exposition

1. We begin with an opening plea (vv. 1–2).
The psalmist begins with four imperatives, all of which call on God to deliver David from those who seek his life. The term *fortress* in verse 1 reappears in verse 16, but there it is a statement of confidence that God truly *is* his fortress even while his house was anything but safe. So, while the psalmist calls on God to be his defense and fortress, the call is set in context of faith and trust that God truly is such.

While the immediate reference to David's enemies is to Saul and his henchmen, as all psalms do, it takes on a larger voice than just that event. Long after David had passed off the scene, the psalm continued to be sung by God's people in worship. As such, the call to God to deliver became of the voice of all worshippers in their own times of crisis and pain. Further, while the enemies in David's context were people, the enemy broadens for the worshippers to anything that creates a threat to them. It could be a person, but it could be a sickness or disease, a relationship, a negative circumstance or event, or more. Today we are free to insert our own story into the psalm and call on God for deliverance. We are invited to call on him to be our fortress in our world and reality. Certainly Martin Luther saw it that way when he composed his classic hymn, "A Mighty Fortress Is Our God."

2. We appeal to God to see and defend us (vv. 3–5).

David is aware of the deadly ambush planned for him by Saul. But David knows he is innocent and has done nothing to deserve this fate. He has been duly anointed by Samuel (see the story in the Prologue from 1 Sam 16:1–13), and has, in fact, shown great deference to Saul as king (eg. 1 Sam 24:1–22). So, David appeals to God from that vantage point. Other psalms express the same idea (eg. Pss 7:3–5, 8; 26:1–12; 139:21–22). Job, too, spends a whole chapter defending his moral, ethical and spiritual innocence (Job 31:1–40). While we all know we are not worthy of the grace shown to us in Jesus Christ—that "all have sinned and fall short of the glory of God" (Rom 3:23) and "We all, like sheep, have gone astray" (Isa 53:6)—there is a place to cry out to God in our times of distress and assert that such brutality, such injustice, such abuse, such pain and suffering, is not deserved. We did nothing to bring it on, and we have a voice of worship in these life realities with which to crash the gates of the throne room of God in prayer.

In somewhat of an unusual move, the psalmist calls God *Yahweh* twice in these verses, which our English Bibles render as *the* LORD. This is worth noting. Book Two of the Book of Psalms (Pss 42–72)[3]

---

[3] The Book of Psalms is divided into five books:

Book One: Psalms 1–41
Book Two: Psalms 42–72 (the Elohistic Psalter)
Book Three: Psalms 73–89
Book Four: Psalms 90–106
Book Five: Psalms 107–150.

This reflects the ongoing development of the book over time, from the time of David to the time of Ezra. It also reflects the five books of the *Torah* (Genesis to Deuteronomy). Some have called the Book of Psalms "the Law in lyric."

is often called the "Elohistic Psalter" because of the dominance of the name *Elohim*, which our English Bibles render as *God*. The name *Elohim* speaks of God's power and strength, while the name *Yahweh* is the covenant name of God given to Moses at the burning bush event (Exod 3:1–15). This little note points the psalmist and us to our God as both a covenant God who keeps faith with his people as well as a God of strength, power and armies.

In this context, as he is being threatened and attacked by his *internal* foe Saul, David takes the idea of attack and threat to the *external* nations. Saul had broken covenant with *Yahweh*, the LORD, and had become like the surrounding nations, something the people had desired from the beginning (cf. 1 Kgs 8:5, 20). Saul had become a traitor to his nation, Israel, and to his anointing as the king of Israel. But as we have noted before, the psalm became the voice of the people long after David and Saul were off the scene. It spoke to the reality of attack and threat coming from any enemy nation, whether the Egyptians, the Assyrians, the Babylonians or others.

The psalm comes to us in the same way now. The psalm has become the voice of the church, beginning in the first century and coming to us in the twenty-first century. We call on God to hear and defend us in the face of nations and people in power who are out to destroy the church—an ever-present reality since the church began and a reality that still exists today. As the seed of Abraham and the inheritor of the covenant made with Abraham (Rom 4:16–17; Gal 3:26–29), we call on God to bless those who bless us and curse those who curse us (cf. Gen 12:2–3).

David boldly calls on God to "rouse yourself." In other words, "to wake up!" In a psalm from the Sons of Korah, they cry out "Awake, Lord! Why do you sleep? Rouse yourself!" (Ps 44:23). Yes, this is bold, and yes we know God never sleeps (Ps 121:4). Elijah mocked the priests of Baal by suggesting their god, Baal, was asleep (1 Kgs 18:27). But, as the voice of God's people to God, there are times when God *seems* silent, hidden or asleep. In Psalm 59 God has given us a voice to allow that feeling to be expressed without guilt or rebuke. It is part of the vast and immense incomprehensibility of our God that shapes our worship of him.[4]

---

[4] There is a *Selah* at the end of this verse and again at the end of verse 13. It is probably some kind of musical term. It occurs 71 times in 39 psalms, including Psalm 52, 57, 59 and 60 in our study. While its meaning is uncertain, many interpreters think it means

Refrain: our enemies are like snarling dogs (vv. 6–7).
This is the first occurrence of this refrain, and it sets the tone for the psalm. David's enemy is compared to a pack of roaming dogs that are vicious and predatory. When humans are compared to dogs in the Bible, it is never a good thing (cf. Deut 23:18; 1 Sam 17:43; 24:14; 2 Sam 16:9; Eccl 9:4). The enemies of David laid wait for him evening after evening. He is in danger and deep distress.

David then expands the metaphor to the vile and violent words the enemy speaks. We can't help but get the idea he is picturing the foaming mouth and sharp teeth of a ravenous dog. Further, not only do they speak with *malice*, David ups the ante and points out that they speak with *impunity*, thinking no one can hear them. But such is not the case. God hears, and later in the psalm he will ask God to ensure that everyone hears their vitriol (vv. 12–13).

3. We affirm our confidence in God (vv. 8–10).
In language that recalls the words of Psalm 2:4, David expresses his confidence that God laughs and scoffs at these enemies. The enemies of God, of God's anointed and of God's people, are no match for the wrath and judgement of Israel's God. This is not a laughter of humour or of uncomfortable embarrassment. It is a laughter of one who is unimpressed, who mocks and scoffs at the nations' petty pride. The reference to nations, as mentioned earlier, refers to Saul and his rule "like the other nations," but it goes beyond Saul to all nations who stand in opposition to God's rule or God's people.

Because of his confidence in God's power against his enemies, David affirms that such power is his strength and his fortress. Earlier he had *appealed* to God to be his fortress, now he *affirms* it. In doing so, he establishes a counter-theme of confidence in the face of the repeated refrain of his enemies coming at him like snarling dogs.

However, deliverance is not yet realized. David waits and watches for God to act. He is like the watchman on the fortress wall who waits and watches, confident deliverance will come but not yet in receipt of it. This is the Christian faith. We find ourselves

---

to pause and reflect, or to rise or stand. The 2011 edition of the NIV does not put the word in the text but rather in the text notes.

in the time between the inauguration of Christ's kingdom and its consummation. While we await his return, we have confidence God is active. He is going before us to accomplish his kingdom and rule, so much so that we can rejoice over the enemy's demise even before it happens (cf. Ps 22:27–28).

4. We appeal to God to expose our enemies (vv. 11–13).

In a fascinating turn, David asks God not to kill his enemy. This is not an indication of mercy. It is actually a call for God to drive the knife in deeper. If God kills his enemy, then the event is over and God's people will forget. That God's people constantly remember his works of deliverance and vindication is a chief concern of Moses (cf. Deut 8:11–20) and the psalmists (cf. Pss 78; 106).

Further, the psalmist wants his enemies uprooted, perhaps similar to what David was experiencing himself, as he was uprooted from his home and had to flee into the wilderness. He wants them brought down—brought down from their pride, power and position, and perhaps even to death.

While there seems to be an over-enthusiastic call for vengeance, the psalmist's ultimate goal is for all peoples everywhere to hear the announcement "God rules over Jacob." The call leans more toward the doxological and less toward the vindictive, although the latter is not absent and to suggest it is absent is naïve.

This is one of many of what are called *imprecations* or calls for curse in the Book of Psalms (eg. Pss 7:6–9; 12:3; 69:22–28; 109:6–15; 137:8–9; 139:19–22). These have been the source of much conversation in psalms studies. Opinions vary widely on how they are to be viewed in Scripture. Some see them as illustrations of inferior spirituality and merely the words of a sinful human psalmist. Others see them as a voice God has given to his people (Israel and the church) to call on him for vindication and justice. While there are many factors that play into this, at the foundation of the call for curse is the covenant made with Abraham mentioned earlier (Gen 12:2–3). The psalmists are calling on God to be true to his covenant, which stated God would bless those who blessed his people and curse those who cursed his people. The call for curse is always referred back to God—"'It is mine to avenge; I will repay,' says the Lord" (Rom 12:19)—and both Jesus and the apostle Paul used similar language (eg. Matt 11:21-24; Luke 10:13-15; Gal 1:8-9).[5]

Refrain: our enemies are like snarling dogs (vv. 14-15).
The "snarling dog" refrain appears a second time. But this time the picture is completed. These dogs are rendered homeless and wanderers as the psalmist has been and will be in times to come. In the first refrain, the dogs are portrayed as vicious, terrifying and acting with impunity. Now they are portrayed as pathetic and constantly on the move for food. A reversal has taken place. The vicious animal has become a wandering and howling creature that has met its demise.

5. We make our final statement of confidence (vv. 16–17).
With a third and fourth reference to *fortress*, the psalmist sings and celebrates God's strength. He has already said God is his strength (v. 9) and now says it again (v. 17). It is God who gives him the strength to resist the enemy, and he brings God's covenantal love into the picture. We cannot help but think of Psalm 46 from the Sons of Korah and their opening words, "God is our refuge and strength, an ever present help in trouble."

In both refrains, the attacking dogs come in the evening. In the story that forms the backdrop for this psalm, Saul's men lay in wait from evening until morning. Even knowing that, David can sing of God's covenantal love that comes in the morning. In spite of the danger surrounding him, he sings praise to God, trusting him as his fortress and strength and affirming God as the One he can rely upon.

So often we are called to trust, sing, praise and live our lives in the context of a world gone awry, where the danger has not yet

---

[5] For a more thorough study of this topic, see David G. Barker, "The Church and Imprecations in the Psalms: The Place of the Call to Curse in the Life of the Church Today," in *Ecclesia Semper Reformanda Est—The Church is Always Reforming: A Festschrift on Ecclesiology in Honour of Stanley K. Fowler*, eds. David G. Barker, Michael A.G. Haykin, Barry H. Howson (Kitchener: Joshua Press, 2016), 65-87. See also John N. Day, *Crying for Justice: What the Psalms Teach Us about Mercy and Vengeance in an Age of Terrorism* (Grand Rapids: Kregel, 2005) and Steffen G. Jenkins, *Imprecations in the Psalms: Love for Enemies in Hard Places* (Eugene: Pickwick, 2022). C.S. Lewis said such imprecations should be completely rejected by Christians. See C.S. Lewis, *Reflections on the Psalms* (London: Harcourt Brace Jovanovich, 1958), 20–22.

passed. Gerald Wilson writes,

> Thus, when the world seems chaotic and beyond control, when our lives seem to disintegrate around us, when the dogs bare their fangs and seek to devour us or carry us away, we need to remember the laughing God, "who is my fortress, my loving God"(59:17).[6]

David sings and prays the psalm while still very much in the *interim*, waiting for deliverance. The people of God in Israel, and later those in the first-century church, also sang it in the interim. We still do so today.

Reflections and lessons

1. What do we learn about God?

(a) While somewhat uncomfortable for us, *we learn God is a laughing God*. He mocks and laughs at humanity's feeble attempts to thwart his kingdom. He especially laughs in the face of arrogant self-confident people. This gives great confidence and hope to those who are victimized by vicious and brutal people because we know that behind his laughter is the power and justice of an impeccably righteous God. We have unwavering confidence in a day when the world will be set to rights, all evil will be conquered (cf. Rev 19:11–21) and a new heavens and earth will come and last for eternity (cf. Isa 65:17–25; Rev 21:1–22:21).

(b) We also learn *God can be called upon to be faithful to his covenantal promises*, particularly the ones to bless and curse as stated in his covenant with Abraham. This imprecatory voice of worship did not end with the Old Testament, as illustrated by Jesus and the apostle Paul. While it is not a voice of petty vengeance for personal vendettas, it is a voice that needs to be heard in the church when God's people, or any person or people for that matter, are the victims of brutality and oppression. While we are to pray for and love our enemies, calling on God to curse the forces of evil arrayed

---

[6] Gerald H. Wilson, *Psalms Volume 1*, NIVAC (Grand Rapids: Zondervan, 2002), 857.

against the church is part of the worshipping voice that the church needs to use.

With great confidence we declare that God is our fortress, refuge and strength in the face of brutal attack. He is the One upon whom we can rely. As such he is worthy of trust and praise.

2. What do we learn about ourselves as the people of God?

Perhaps it comes as a bit of a surprise to us, but as the people of God we have the right to appeal to God as those who are innocent and undeserving of the difficulties we face. Yes, we are sinful and unworthy of the grace we have received in Christ; but as noted above, the psalms regularly come from the voice of psalmists protesting their innocence. Job, too, was vehement in his protests (eg. Job 3:1–26; 29:14; 31:1–40), and in the end was vindicated by God with the powerful words "my servant Job" stated four times (Job 42:7–8). Yes, Job repented "in dust and ashes" (Job 42:6), but that was not for any sin or sinfulness, but for an inadequate view of the power and presence of God. We are all subject to that kind of repentance because of our miniscule view of the fullness of the nature of God (cf. Rom 11:33–36). But God hears us in our protests of innocence, and we can trust him to act in mercy and love on our behalf. However, when we pray such a psalm from a vantage point of innocence, we need to ensure we are examining our lives to ensure we are living faithfully for God. Job, time and time again, made it explicit that he was living a life of faithfulness in his protests against his "friends" who cycled back again and again to accusations of sin and failure as the reasons God was inflicting him with suffering (eg. Job 6:24–30).

We have a voice to call on God to wake up! Yes, we know he never sleeps (Ps 121:4), but there are times when we think he is. He is big enough in himself to hear our call for him to "rouse yourself." This gives an authenticity to our prayers and songs that goes deep into the realities of the life we all live. While we don't come to God with impunity (Pss 1 and 2 are the gateposts we pass through to enter the world of the Psalms[7]), we do come

---

[7] Eugene Peterson says that as we enter the Book of Psalms, Psalm 1 brings us to *attention* and Psalm 2 brings us to *adoration*. See Eugene Peterson, *Answering God: The Psalms as Tools for Prayer* (New York: HarperCollins, 1989), 23–32.

boldly and are welcomed by God. As any parent would do, he welcomes his children to run to him with bared hearts and the cries of frustration—even with him—in our pain and loss.

3. What do we learn about the world?
We learn that the world can be a vicious and brutal place. It is not always that way, but it can be, and we have a voice. But we also learn *the world is under the sovereign rule of God.* Whether extending life to the forces of evil so that God's people will not forget, or displaying such forces as his conquest, or bringing the forces of evil to nothing or even laughing at them, God rules over his own people and the nations. We can know that ultimately and finally the nations will know the power, justice and rule of God.

Final word
We referred earlier to Martin Luther's classic hymn, "A Mighty Fortress Is Our God." While probably rooted in Psalm 46:1, it speaks to the same confidence we find in Psalm 59.

> A mighty fortress is our God,
>   a bulwark never failing;
> our helper he amid the flood
>   of mortal ills prevailing.
> For still our ancient foe
>   doth seek to work us woe;
> his craft and power are great,
>   and armed with cruel hate,
>   on earth is not his equal.
>
> Did we in our own strength confide,
>   our striving would be losing,
> were not the right man on our side,
>   the man of God's own choosing.
> Dost ask who that may be?
>   Christ Jesus, it is he;
> Lord Sabaoth, his name,
>   from age to age the same,
>   and he must win the battle.

And though this world, with devils filled,
    should threaten to undo us,
we will not fear, for God hath willed
    his truth to triumph through us.
The Prince of Darkness grim,
    we tremble not for him;
his rage we can endure,
    for lo, his doom is sure;
    one little word shall fell him.

That word above all earthly powers,
    no thanks to them, abideth;
the Spirit and the gifts are ours,
    thru him who with us sideth.
Let goods and kindred go,
    this mortal life also;
the body they may kill;
    God's truth abideth still;
    his kingdom is forever.[8]

---

[8] Martin Luther, "A Mighty Fortress Is Our God," Public Domain, 1529.

CHAPTER 2

GRATITUDE WHEN THINGS GO BIZARRE

BIBLE READING
1 Samuel 21:10–15
Psalm 34

Story ♦ 1 Samuel 21:10–15

I didn't like it. I didn't like it from the day that fugitive came to our city of Gath. A fugitive who came to our city and sought protection from our esteemed King Achish. I said to my king, "This is not good. There is something about this guy I don't like. There is something rotten in Gath. We don't want him here."

So, my esteemed king sent me on a mission—a mission of espionage. "Follow him. Watch him. Listen to him," the king said to me. So, I followed and watched him for several days. He blended in well with our people. He stayed out of public places. He was essentially invisible.

We knew he was hiding. We knew he was frightened of something or someone. But I needed to find out, not just for my king, but to confirm my own suspicion, the thing which caused the stake-out in the first place. For days, I could learn nothing. He played the part well.

Finally, things turned my way. Three things gave him away, although I was pretty dense as to the first one. It was this: *the sword*! All along I thought it was too big for the man, but I never twigged as to why or what it was. Then I got a closer look. When I realized what I was looking at, it rocked my world. It was the sword of our giant hero—Goliath. The sword of our giant hero who had been so horribly defeated by a Hebrew shepherd boy. The story was well known in our city. Goliath was our frontline warrior. He had been defeated by a shepherd boy with a slingshot. The humiliation and defeat was almost unbearable. Their own king, a big man himself, had refused to do battle. From what we had heard, this shepherd boy, while visiting his brothers in the Israelite army, saw our Goliath defying their king and their God, and volunteered to take him on! So, alone, no armour, a slingshot and some stones in his shepherd's pouch, calling on the name of his God *Yahweh*, he felled our giant warrior with a single rock to the head. It was a rout after that. The Israelite army chased us back into two of our cities, Gath and Ekron, and the boy decapitated our hero with his own sword.

We never knew where the sword went. And now, here it is, in our city, Goliath's own city, strapped to the side of this fugitive. How he ever knew where it was and how he ever got it, I don't think we'll ever know.[1]

The second hint came when I heard him speak. He spoke our language, for sure. We know it as Canaanite. But we Philistines, also known as the Sea Peoples, were immigrants into the area 250 years ago from the west end of the Great Sea. Canaanite was not our native language. Over the years, we learned the language of Canaan where we now lived. But we have a distinctive accent. And this gave him away. This man spoke native Canaanite, or Hebrew as it had become known, because the dominant nation who spoke it were known as Hebrews.[2] So, this fugitive was not a Philistine—one of us. He was evidently a Hebrew, an Israelite, our enemy. And he was wearing Goliath's sword, in Gath, Goliath's city!

And then the third piece. We actually found out who he was. I was gobsmacked. He was David ben-Jesse! That was the name of the

---

[1] David came across the sword in a shrine in a place called Nob, northeast of Jerusalem (1 Sam 21:9).

[2] We know there were distinctive accents among Canaanite speakers, as illustrated by the Ephraimites pronouncing the word *Shibboleth* as *Sibboleth* (cf. Judg 12:6).

shepherd boy who had taken out our hero Goliath just a few short years ago. We had heard that this David, Goliath's killer, had been secretly anointed king of the Hebrews by a holy man of theirs named Samuel. We heard he was on the lam, running from their king, Saul ben-Kish, who was not happy with him. David had married the king's daughter and so was his son-in-law. He was also a close friend of the king's son, which infuriated King Saul even more. And now, here David was, hiding out among us, wearing Goliath's sword. This was not good.

So, with all these pieces in place I made a mad dash to King Achish, asked for an immediate audience with him, which was granted, and I gasped out the story. Then I asked him point blank, "Isn't this David, the king of the land? Isn't this the one they sing about in their dances, 'Saul has slain his thousands, and David his tens of thousands?'"

King Achish also quickly realized, as I did, this was not good. He realized David is the man who had already defeated our hero giant. Further, he realized this is the man that killed 200 of his people in order to prove himself worthy to marry the king's daughter. Yes, David had killed 200 of our countrymen! But their King Saul, the king of the Hebrews, was after him. If King Saul found him in the city of Gath, well, it was not going to end well for the city, and for himself as king of the city.

So, that was enough for our king. Immediately, he sent a posse of armed men and brought in this David ben-Jesse. But now, the story takes a bizarre turn. The guy went insane! He went out of his mind in the palace, in the presence of our esteemed King Achish. It was unbelievable—spittle dripping down his beard, a wild look in his eyes, scraping the door posts with his fingernails leaving blood and scratches on them, babbling incoherently. He went completely mad in front of our eyes. We had no idea what happened. Was it an act? If it was, it was a dangerous one. Our king was well known for executing anyone he did not view as valuable. Was it a collapse of the brain because of the pressure of all he was facing? Further, it was brutally humiliating for him, and for the God he claimed to worship (although I have no idea why he would be doing what he was doing if he truly worshipped and trusted the God he said he worshipped). We laughed. We mocked. We teased. But finally King Achish had enough. He said, "Look at the man! He is insane! Why bring him to me? Am I so short of madmen that you have to bring this fellow here to carry on like this? Must this man come into my house?"

So, with that (and his life spared) we dragged him to the edge of the city, pushed him out of the gate, and sent him on his way still ranting, raving and drooling down his beard like a madman. We did hear he wound up in some cave in the foothills that belonged to someone by the name of Adullam. We also found out later that, yes, it was an act, a really good one, and he had became the leader of a band of guerrilla fighters. Further, we soon discovered it wouldn't be the last time we would have to deal with him. In fact, when we look back, we should have terminated him when we had the chance. We blew it, badly.

So, I am not sure what to think about all this. These Hebrews, or Israelites as they are sometimes called, claim their God, the God they call *Yahweh*, is the supreme and only God of the heavens. His mere name means "he is" and he defies all other gods, including our revered god Dagon. So, this *Yahweh* worshipper, on the run from his king (and father-in-law), comes and hides in *our* city! Where is his confidence in his God? Is he trying to be Goliath? The sword, the city—of Goliath! Is this panic? This seems to be a complete reversal. When he fought our hero giant, he clearly said in a voice we could all hear:

> You come against me with sword and spear and javelin, but I come against you in the name of the LORD Almighty, the God of the armies of Israel, whom you have defied. This day the LORD will deliver you into my hands, and I'll strike you down and cut off your head. This very day I will deliver the carcasses of the Philistine army to the birds and the wild animals and the whole world will know that there is a God in Israel. All those gathered here will know that it is not by sword or spear that the LORD saves; for the battle is the LORD's, and he will give all of you into my hands.

But now he hides among us with a sword—Goliath's sword—and shows no faith or confidence in his God. We mock him. We laugh! We mock his God as well! How can this be a declaration that "the whole world will know that there is a God in Israel"? I can only conclude he has failed in his faith and lost confidence in his God. Yes, he got out with his life. I guess I can say his God delivered him. But, I have to think that it was more in spite of David ben-Jesse's faith than because of it. Oh well, I guess I'll just stay with my god, the revered Dagon. Their God does not seem to be a God his worshippers can trust.

Song ◆ Psalm 34

Of David. When he pretended to be insane before Abimelek, who drove him away, and he left.

1 I will extol the LORD at all times;
    his praise will always be on my lips.
2 I will glory in the LORD;
    let the afflicted hear and rejoice.
3 Glorify the LORD with me;
    let us exalt his name together.

4 I sought the LORD, and he answered me;
    he delivered me from all my fears.
5 Those who look to him are radiant;
    their faces are never covered with shame.
6 This poor man called, and the LORD heard him;
    he saved him out of all his troubles.
7 The angel of the LORD encamps around those who fear him,
    and he delivers them.

8 Taste and see that the LORD is good;
    blessed is the one who takes refuge in him.
9 Fear the LORD, you his holy people,
    for those who fear him lack nothing.
10 The lions may grow weak and hungry,
    but those who seek the LORD lack no good thing.
11 Come, my children, listen to me;
    I will teach you the fear of the LORD.
12 Whoever of you loves life
    and desires to see many good days,
13 keep your tongue from evil
    and your lips from telling lies.
14 Turn from evil and do good;
    seek peace and pursue it.

15 The eyes of the LORD are on the righteous,
    and his ears are attentive to their cry;
16 but the face of the LORD is against those who do evil,

to blot out their name from the earth.

17 The righteous cry out, and the LORD hears them;
    he delivers them from all their troubles.
18 The LORD is close to the brokenhearted
    and saves those who are crushed in spirit.

19 The righteous person may have many troubles,
    but the LORD delivers him from them all;
20 he protects all his bones,
    not one of them will be broken.

21 Evil will slay the wicked;
    the foes of the righteous will be condemned.
22 The LORD will rescue his servants;
    no one who takes refuge in him will be condemned.

Introductory notes

Out of a story of faking and faithlessness comes one of the most beautiful expressions of gratitude, piety, wisdom and praise of God we have anywhere in the Book of Psalms. The story does not seem to blend with the psalm. In fact, we could say that if David truly believed what he said in the psalm he would never have done what he did in Gath. So, the psalm seems to be a post-event reflection by David, as he thinks back on that event and realizes how gracious God was to him in spite of his bizarre and shameful actions.[3]

1. The king named in the title is Abimelek.

In 1 Samuel 21:10–15 he is named *Achish*. It seems that *Abimelek* is more of a Philistine dynastic title similar to the word *Pharaoh*, while *Achish* is his personal name. We see the word used of Philistine kings in two places in the Old Testament. The first is in Genesis 20

---

[3] Some read this story differently and suggest this was God's way of getting his faithful servant out of a difficult situation. It might be compared to the Hebrew midwives lying to Pharaoh (Exod 1:19) or Samson violating Hebrew law in demanding a Philistine wife but which was "from the LORD, who was seeking an occasion to confront the Philistines" (Judg 14:4). It is interesting that later David and his men settle in Gath for over a year with Achish's blessing (1 Sam 27:1–7). To read it in this way minimizes the contrast between the story and psalm.

where Abimelek, king of the Philistine city Gerar, tried to take Sarah, Abraham's wife, into his harem. Abraham had lied about Sarah and called her his sister. Because of her beauty he was afraid he would be killed so that someone like Abimelek could take Sarah as his wife. The second time we see the name used is in Genesis 26 in a similar event with Isaac and Rebekah. It's a later Abimelek who was now king in Gath, one of the five Philistine cities.[4]

The name *Abimelek* also occurs in the story of Gideon. He is one of Gideon's sons. The name means "my father is king" and evidently Gideon gave him that name to indicate his desire to start a family dynasty even though he denied such an intent (Judg 8:22–24). The name also occurs in 1 Chronicles 18:16 for a priest in David's day. However, it is most likely a misspelling or a variant on the name *Ahimelek*.

2. The psalm is categorized as a thanksgiving psalm.

A thanksgiving psalm is differentiated from a praise psalm in that it reviews the difficulty the psalmist has experienced and celebrates God's deliverance from that difficult circumstance. While a praise psalm is what we call a *psalm of orientation* and a lament psalm is a *psalm of disorientation*, a thanksgiving psalm is a *psalm of reorientation*—a psalm that takes the disorientation and moves it to a new sense of orientation.[5] The psalm also has a wisdom element in it. In verses 8–14, David becomes a teacher and teaches the reader to "fear the LORD," a classic characteristic of wisdom literature in general.

3. The psalm is an acrostic psalm.

An interesting characteristic of the psalm is that it has twenty-two verses, the same number as the Hebrew alphabet, and each verse

---

[4] Both these references are anachronistic since the Sea Peoples, who many think are the ancestors of the Philistines, did not settle on the coast until the thirteenth century B.C. The patriarchal events happened several centuries earlier. It is evident in the book of Genesis that Moses or a later editor used the *current* name of the occupants of that area to tell the patriarchal stories.

[5] Walter Brueggemann has come up with these terms to describe many of the psalms. See Walter Brueggemann, *The Message of the Psalms: A Theological Commentary* (Minneapolis: Augsburg, 1984), 21. Not everyone likes his approach, since for some it reflects more of a psychological approach rather than a theological one. See Bruce K. Waltke, James M. Houston and Erika Moore, *The Psalms as Christian Lament: A Historical Commentary* (Grand Rapids: Eerdmans, 2014), 3-4, who call it "a revolt against biblical orthodoxy."

follows the sequence of the alphabet.[6] As such it is called an *acrostic* psalm. There are several psalms that follow this pattern to a greater or lesser extent (Pss 25; 37; 111; 112; 145) and the classic example is Psalm 119, which has twenty-two stanzas of eight verses each following the Hebrew alphabet. We also see acrostic poems in Proverbs 31:10–31 and Lamentations 1–3 (sixty-six verses) and 4 (not chapter 5 even though it is twenty-two verses long).

The point of an acrostic poem is twofold. First, it seems to be a mnemonic device aiding the memorization of the poem. Second, it seems to reflect completeness, going from A to Z as it were. This psalm would have been well known in the temple and synagogue, and later in the early church. It is a strong and literarily complete statement of thanksgiving for God's grace and care for his people. It certainly has become one of the most well known psalms in the church today.

Outline of the psalm
Psalm 34 has six parts:

1. A proclamation of praise (vv. 1–3)
2. A personal testimony (vv. 4–7)
3. An instruction in wisdom (vv. 8–14)
4. An assurance of God's care (vv. 15–18)
5. An assurance of God's protection (vv. 19–21)
6. An assurance of God's redemption (v. 22)

Message of the psalm
In Psalm 34, in the context of danger and misguided action, we hear praise to God for his gracious deliverance in answer to the desperate prayers of his people. We also hear the teaching that God's people are called to turn from evil and pursue godliness and the fear of the Lord, since God sees, hears and delivers the righteous and brokenhearted.

---

[6] However, it is somewhat irregular in that it lacks a verse for the *vav* letter and adds a crucial verse outside the acrostic at the end to get to twenty-two verses. The final verse outside the acrostic concludes the psalm with a resounding assurance of God's rescue.

Exposition

1. We are called to be a people that bless God in affliction (vv. 1–3).

In the context of the bizarre circumstance of this psalm, David starts by declaring that he will extol and praise the Lord in all times and circumstances. This seems to be in serious conflict with the historical reality behind the psalm. David is in deep trouble and he is not dealing with it well. Throughout the Psalter, lament psalms give a legitimate voice of worship in times of trouble, and so it is important that to understand this psalm, it ought to be read in conjunction with Psalms 13 and 44, and even the next one, Psalm 35. But what this psalm does is help us understand that while life is often muddled and messy, in the end it is supervised by God. We rest in the knowledge that things are not out of control and somehow God's will and ways are being worked out.

The word *extol* comes from the Hebrew word *barakh*, which is most often translated *bless*. It carries the idea of referring all of life back to God in an act and attitude of affirming and honouring God. It expresses pleasure and satisfaction no matter what life brings. It is paralleled with the word *praise*, which reinforces this idea. In verses 2 and 3, David goes on to affirm that he will praise the Lord, and he calls upon God's people to lift up, honour and glorify the Lord.

So, while this psalm seems out of step with the realities of David's life (and often ours), these opening verses remind us of two things. They remind us we need to read *all* the psalms. Lament psalms give us voice to express our pain and loss, but a psalm like this, set in broken circumstances, picks up on the inevitable ending of lament psalms—the vow to praise or a testimony of God's goodness. While David talks about "at all times," I think we need to acknowledge that sometimes it takes some time to get there. We walk slowly in the journey to praise, and we need to allow others to do the same.

Further, Psalm 34 reminds us that gratitude and praise are often a *decision*. A similar situation is found in Psalm 57, where David points us to the reality that praise of God is often set in the context of being "in the midst of lions." We are often called to *choose* gratitude, even when it is difficult to do so. Both Psalms 34:3 and 57:5, 7—popular lines in contemporary worship music—are set in contexts of difficulty. They need to be sung and read in light of the entire Book of Psalms and understood in the circumstances in which they are found.

2. We are called to announce God's nearness and care (vv. 4–7).

Since David asserts he sought the Lord and the Lord answered him, we need to believe it happened. Evidently, behind that act of feigned insanity, he called on God for help. I wonder if David had any regrets for choosing to act the way he did. What these verses do is help me know that even when I take things into my own hands, and at times really mess things up, God never abandons me. In my desperation, often as a result of my own actions, he hears and answers and, at least for David, delivers.

Was David's face covered with shame? Well, it would seem so, at least in front of Abimelek. But we hear that in the presence of God, even when we have not done well, he smiles on us and we can look to him in confidence. He does not shake his finger at us and say, "Shame on you, shame on you." In fact, we can be "radiant" before God, a term used to describe the face of a mother when she finds a lost child (Isa 60:5). It is also the term used to describe Moses' face after his encounter with God on Mount Sinai (Exod 34:29). This takes us to a whole new level in our confidence and rest in the grace and mercy of our God (cf. 2 Cor 3:18).

With David, we as "poor" people, call out to God and he hears us.[7] Three times in this psalm David announces that he and God's people will be saved out of all their troubles (vv. 6, 17, 19). Yes, for David, he was saved out those troubles in Gath. However, far too often we are *not* saved out of all our troubles. Health issues, broken relationships and difficult circumstances persist.

So, how are we to understand such a strong affirmation by David? Two things seem to be in play here. First, this is *poetry*, and poetry tends toward hyperbole and the ideal. We use poetry to express the extreme, whether our love for someone, our pain in loss or our hope in difficulty. So, we read this as such.

Second, the statement is *ultimately* true. There *is* a day coming when we will be delivered from all our troubles. It's called the new

---

[7] This is the source of the title of this book.

heavens and new earth. While we most often go to Revelation 21:1–5 to hear these promises, we need to remember that the apostle John was building off the beautiful description of the new heavens and new earth in Isaiah 65:17–25. In Isaiah's description, there will be no more weeping (v. 19) and no more hurting and destroying (v. 25).[8] While Isaiah lived several hundred years after David, this concept is part of the theology of God's people throughout the Old Testament. We need not think that David and others could not have had this awareness in their thinking and writing. And, with both Isaiah and John as part of our theology of hope, we too can look to that glorious day when we will be delivered from all our troubles and all our enemies will be destroyed. We need to embrace those sure and certain promises of future deliverance to fully understand and enter into the words of this psalm and others like it.

The "angel of the LORD" is a common idea in the Old Testament. It regularly refers to the presence of God, or a messenger of God, in the life and circumstances of his people.[9] Whatever David understood by this idea, it reminds us that God is never far away from his people—those who "fear" him can be sure of deliverance. For David, it was from Abimelek/Achish. For us, it may be in this life and time, and if not now, in that future day to come.

I find it challenging and encouraging to think Psalm 34 was accepted by the people of God as worthy of inclusion in the Psalter set in the context of the title (irrespective of when that title was added, see Introduction). On one level, it seems almost hypocritical for David to express this kind of piety in the setting of Gath. But the Israelite community of faith, and later the church, accepted it as part of the Psalter as an authentic expression of worship, even in the conflicting circumstances on which the psalm was based. This voice has now become our voice, and it brings that same sense of confidence for us as it did for them.

---

[8] This description of the new heavens and earth is set in the context of Israel's return from exile in Babylon, but clearly it has futuristic overtones and John in Revelation takes it that way (Rev 21:4).

[9] For a helpful study on "the angel of the LORD," see Craig A. Carter, "Just Another Angel? The Angel of the LORD and the Doctrine of the Trinity," *Reading Scripture, Learning Wisdom: Essays in Honour of David G. Barker*, eds. Michael A.G. Haykin and Barry H. Howson (Peterborough: Joshua Press, 2021), 61–75.

3. We are instructed in wisdom (vv. 8–14).

Now David takes on the role of a *sage* teaching his people wisdom. The sage in Israel brought godly wisdom out of the experiences of life, good and bad. This was one of three *pastoral* voices that spoke into the community. The other two are the *prophets*, with their calls to covenantal loyalty and justice, and *priests*, with their teaching of the law and their leadership in worship (cf. Jer 18:18; Ezek 7:26). While these three roles are not part of official church structure today, I am convinced that all three voices still need to be heard in the church today.

The word *insane* in the title is the same word as *taste* in verse 8, and may be part of the reason this title was placed at the head of this psalm. There seems to be an almost comic play on words with the title reading, "Of David. When he altered his *taste* before Abimelek."

David picks up on two common characteristics of biblical wisdom. First, he announces that the person who takes refuge in God is *blessed* by God. While it is often thought that the word should be translated as *happy*, *blessed* reflects a more sober and thoughtful meaning that speaks of the smile of God on someone, and the contentedness and tranquility such a smile brings. Then, twice David talks about the "fear of the LORD," the central focus of what it means to live a wise life (cf. Prov 9:10; Eccl 12:13–14). The phrase is a worship phrase that speaks to bringing all we know about God—his glory, grace, love, mercy, justice, righteousness, and more—to the central orbit of our lives, wrapping our lives around him and all that he is. It is a *theocentric* phrase that puts God—his will, ways, values, glory and mission—at the heart of our lives.

From David the sage, we learn that when we taste, seek, fear and find refuge in the Lord, as his holy people, the smile and favour of God rests on our lives. As a result, we lack nothing, no good thing. Again, this is not the promise of a life of ease and prosperity. It is a poetic and idealistic promise, assuring us that all the resources we need to live our lives of faith are available from our God. Lions, beasts of power and danger, do not have the same place in the care of God as his people have.

So, we hear David call. He calls his children (Israel), and us. We are learning wisdom from someone who has experienced the challenges of life in both faith and failure. There is an authenticity that gives us both an ear to listen and a cause to hope in our God.

Gratitude when things go bizarre

If David can emerge from this scene in Gath with this kind of wisdom, truly it is teaching we need to embrace.

David articulates three things we need to bring to the table (vv. 13–14):

a. Keep our tongues/words under control and centred on truth
b. Turn from evil and always do good
c. Seek and pursue peace

The wisdom teachers of the Old Testament often gave instructions about the tongue (eg. Prov 10:19; 12:18). In the New Testament, James notes the importance of controlling the tongue (Jas 1:26; 3:3–6). Further, turning from evil is central to what a follower of God in Christ is to pursue (Rom 12:9). The apostle Paul called the church to be characterized by doing good (Gal 6:9–10). And, we cannot help but hear Jesus' words, "Blessed are the peacemakers," in his famous Sermon on the Mount (Matt 5:9). Paul, likewise, instructs those in the church to be agents of peace (Rom 12:18; 1 Thess 5:13).

4. We are assured of God's care (vv. 15–18).

While there have been brief allusions earlier in the psalm to the fact that David is in trouble (v. 6), I have noted that the doxological tenor of the psalm seems to be at odds with his circumstances in Gath. Now, however, David acknowledges that things are not good for him. There is a cry (v. 17) followed by wonderful assurance that God hears the cry and is near to those languishing in their troubles.

It is true that God does not literally have eyes, ears and a face (vv. 15–16). But using these personifications brings the reality of God's presence and care into a concrete form for David, and, because of that, he experiences an even more intense and meaningful relationship with God. The image of God's "face" throughout the Psalms is one of both despair and blessing. When God *hides* his face from his people there is a deep sense of loss and abandonment (Pss 30:7; 104:29) and a common cry of the psalmists is "Why do you hide your face?" (Pss 30:7; 44:24; 88:14). But when God's face is *turned* toward his people, there is blessing and hope, reflecting the words of the Aaronic benediction (Num 6:25–26; Pss 4:6; 67:1). In this case, David turns the image of God's face *against* his enemies, the ones doing evil against him, and declares the memory of them terminated from the earth.

On the other hand, when the *righteous*—one of several terms for God's people in the Psalms and throughout the Old Testament (see v. 19 below)—cry out, the Lord hears them, delivers them, is close to them and saves them. These words taken together give massive assurance to the faithful people of God that he will never abandon us in our trouble and despair or when we are brokenhearted and crushed in spirit. This is true even when the trouble may be caused by our own doing, as it was for David.

5. We are assured of God's protection (vv. 19–21).

In typical wisdom style, the fate of the righteous and the wicked are contrasted. The righteous will be delivered from their "many troubles" but the wicked will be condemned and slain. It is interesting that it is *evil itself* that will slay the wicked. The evil acts of the wicked come full circle and become the agents of their death.

Four times in verses 15–21, God's people are called *righteous*. Some translate it *faithful*, which is also a valid rendering. This is a common term used for God's people throughout the Psalms and the Old Testament as a whole. It does not necessarily speak of personal morality or righteousness that we tend to think of, or even the theological concept of the apostle Paul and the New Testament of being "declared" righteous. Rather, it is a *relational* term that identifies a community of people in covenant relationship to God, in contrast to the enemy who is evil and outside the covenant. The righteous are those who live in the fear of the LORD (vv. 7, 9, 11), take refuge in the LORD (v. 8) and seek the LORD (v. 10).

Verse 20 is quoted of Jesus by the apostle John in John 19:36. While I would not interpret this as a direct psalmic prophecy of Jesus,[10] John affirms Jesus is the *ultimate* righteous man and applies the statement to him. Jesus was the only one of the three on those Roman crosses whose legs were not broken (John 19:33). Further, the apostle John may well be making an allusion to Exodus 12:46, which states that no bones of the Passover lamb were to be broken.

---

[10] Waltke identifies this text, along with Psalm 2:1–6 and 22:18, as "typico-prophetic." He writes: "David's sufferings and glory typify Jesus Christ, but sometimes his language transcends his own personal experience and finds its fulfillment in Jesus Christ," Waltke *et al, The Psalms as Christian Worship*, 112.

However, the statement in the psalm has immediate application to David and the readers of his day. It continues to give reassurance of God's protection to God's people of all times. But is it true that none of the bones of the righteous will be broken? Of course, we know this is not so. Many of God's people have had their bones broken, and worse, by the wicked. As noted earlier, we are in the domain of the poetic and hyperbole. We hear this statement as the poetry it is, in the same way we hear the confidence of David that the righteous will be delivered from all their troubles.

6. We are assured of God's redemption (v. 22).

We come to the final verse in the psalm and it stands outside the acrostic. David has chosen to use this technique to draw our attention to his final and climactic conclusion. Yes, David was rescued, perhaps by bizarre means, but he can now refer it back to God. This does not justify his actions, but it does show how God often takes the tangled threads of our lives and brings order out of the chaos we have created for ourselves.

Further, in this verse he uses the word *servants* to speak of God's people. To be called the servant of God is a term of deep endearment and intense relationship. It is used of Moses (Num 12:7), Samuel (1 Sam 3:10), Job (Job 1:8; 42:7–8), the nation of Israel itself (Isa 41:8) and ultimately Jesus the Messiah (Isa 42:1–9; 49:1–13; 50:4–11; 52:13–53:12; cf. Matt 12:18–21; John 12:38; Rom 10:16). The identity of God's people has now moved from the *righteous* to *servant*, with both terms connected to Christ. This is powerful language and speaks to our relationship to God grounded in care, protection and rescue.

David goes back to verse 8 where he affirmed the blessedness of those who take refuge in the Lord. Now, he states the contrasting side of taking such refuge: "no one who takes refuge in him will be condemned." He has just used the word *condemned* in the previous verse to speak of the enemies of the righteous and how evil will destroy them. Now he states that such condemnation is *not* the destiny of God's servants. We cannot help but think of the apostle Paul's words, "Therefore, there is now no condemnation for those who are in Christ Jesus" (Rom 8:1).

Reflections and lessons

1. What do we learn about God?

(a) In the stories in the Bible, *we look for God to be the hero of the story*. In this story, he seems completely absent. There is no mention of God anywhere. David has taken things into his own hands and the result is disastrous. I am reminded of the book of Esther in which the name of God is never mentioned. But God was faithful to his people then, even as he is to David here. We also see this in Hosea. Hosea, as the husband of Gomer, is a symbol of God as a husband to his people Israel. When Hosea restores his wayward wife Gomer, it is symbolizing God's restoration of his wayward people. Our covenant God never abandons his people.

(b) We also see that *God lets us go our own way and experience the messes that inevitably develop*. As a result, yes, God may exile his people for a time (even as David was "exiled" in Gath). But in the end, *ultimately*, he rescues, returns and restores his people. While David resorted to a shameful means of escape, he concludes, "The LORD will rescue his servants; no one who takes refuge in him will be condemned" (v. 22). In the end, David realizes *it was God* who got him out of Gath.

2. What do we learn about ourselves as the people of God?

The primary thing that strikes me in the story is how far a hero of faith can fall. David had done great exploits in the name of his God. To stand up to Goliath with a slingshot and defy the giant in the name of the Lord was an outstanding act of faith. Yet here he is, with Goliath's sword in Gath, hiding from Saul and reduced to acting like a clown to escape. It is a warning to us all. We are never beyond the need for daily faith, humble dependence and ongoing obedience. This story has been lived out over and over again in the history of the church, with tragic consequences for the person involved, the people of God and the testimony of God himself.

A second thing we learn is that when we take things into our own hands, thinking we know the best way out, even as David did in deciding to hide in Gath with Goliath's sword, we inevitably make things worse. In a later story, David will do the opposite and not kill

Saul in a cave when he had a chance. Perhaps David learned from his mistake in Gath and recognized that staying in the will and ways of God was the best path forward for himself and his followers.

The last verse of the psalm is riveting. The first line points us to the *grace* of God and the *cost* of such rescue. The second line points us to the glorious *result*. Derek Kidner writes, "The Christian can echo the jubilant spirit of the psalm with added gratitude, knowing the unimagined cost of 22a and the unbounded scope of 22b."[11]

3. What do we learn about the world?

Achish captures the words of the world, "Am I so short of madmen that you have to bring this fellow here to carry on like this in front of me?" (1 Sam 21:15). The world mocks when Christians fail in faith and humility. They mock us, and inevitably our God. How many times have we engaged in an awkward conversation with a neighbour after the headlines announce the massive failure of a Christian leader?

At the same time, none of us are immune. We all can be David. Whether we are a prominent leader or a quiet servant in the church, our actions have consequences. The world sees and hears, and the mission of the gospel is deeply affected.

David found out that Gath, a Gentile Philistine city, was a place of false security and even danger. Centuries earlier, in a story that David certainly knew, his forefather Jacob had turned west at the Jabbok River and settled in the hills just outside the Canaanite city of Shechem. He did this instead of following his brother Esau back to Hebron, the home of his family, as he had promised. As a result, disaster struck (see Gen 33–34). While we all live in "the world," and yes, there is much good and beauty in the world, if we deliberately use that world as our hiding place, security and moral definition, as Jeremiah says, "Death has climbed in through our windows" (Jer 9:21).

Final word

Psalm 34 emerges from one of the most bizarre stories in Scripture, and as I have noted several times, the story seems so at odds with

---

[11] Derek Kidner, *Psalms 1–72*, Tyndale Old Testament Commentaries (Downers Grove: InterVarsity, 1973), 142.

the sentiment of the psalm. But, in many ways, this helps us pray the psalms with authenticity and faith. Whether we understand or even experience the reality of a particular psalm, we need to pray them all with this end in view: to make use of them as our prayers so that, in faith, we surrender ourselves to God, our King.

The legacy of this psalm is captured in the hymn "Through All the Changing Scenes of Life":

> Through all the changing scenes of life,
>   In trouble and in joy,
> The praises of my God shall still
>   My heart and tongue employ.
>
> Oh, magnify the Lord with me,
>   With me exalt His name;
> When in distress to Him I called,
>   He to my rescue came.
>
> The hosts of God encamp around
>   The dwellings of the just;
> Deliverance He affords to all
>   Who on His succor trust.
>
> Oh, make but trial of His love,
>   Experience will decide
> How blest they are, and only they,
>   Who in His truth confide.
>
> Fear Him, ye saints, and you will then
>   Have nothing else to fear;
> Make you His service your delight,
>   Your wants shall be His care.[12]

---

[12] Nahum Brady and Nicholas Tate, "Through All the Changing Scenes of Life," Public Domain, 1696.

CHAPTER 3

CONFIDENCE IN THE FACE OF BETRAYAL

BIBLE READING
1 Samuel 21:1–9; 22:6–13
Psalm 52

Story ◆ 1 Samuel 21:1–9; 22:6–13

It was one of the most horrific events of my life. Eight-five priests dead, my father dead and the whole village put to the sword by one man named Doeg from Edom. I escaped. I fled to the fugitive David, who was himself fleeing from King Saul. He told me I would be safe with him.

My name is Abiathar and I am the son of a priest named Ahimelech who was in charge of the tabernacle located at this time in the village of Nob, just north of Jerusalem. We are in chaotic times. King Saul, the king chosen by our people because of his powerful presence and good looks, a king "like the other nations," as we said we wanted, has been rejected by our God. A shepherd boy named David, the youngest of eight sons of Jesse from Bethlehem, has been quietly anointed as king by the venerable prophet Samuel. King Saul has met this news with blinding fury, empowered by an evil spirit placed on him by God.

Now King Saul is on the hunt for David and David is on the run. One day, desperate for food and weapons, David came to the tabernacle at Nob. He was also looking for a word of guidance from God from the Urim and Thummim. These are dice-like objects which were carried in the breastplate of my father's ephod, a coat he wore when he was doing his priestly duties. I remember that event. David came alone, which was a little unusual since he did have a band of loyal followers who were on the run with him. My father asked him why he came alone. For some reason, David lied. He said Saul had sent him with a mission no one was to know about. Why David deceived my father, no one knows. Our best guess is he was trying to protect my father from a king who David knew would be ruthless to anyone who gave him protection or refuge. If that was the reason, it didn't work, as the rest of my story will tell you. He also told my father he was going to meet his men at an undisclosed place. Again, perhaps the secrecy was to protect my father.

My father told David he didn't have any food except the consecrated bread that was in the Holy Place, the first room of the tabernacle. This bread was replaced with fresh loaves every day. According to the law of Moses, the replaced bread could only be eaten by the priests. But because of the desperate plight of David, and the fact that the law of Moses allowed for acts of mercy,[1] my father gave David the consecrated bread for him and his men. The only condition was they were to be ceremonially clean, meaning they had not had sexual relations the previous night and would keep themselves from women until sunset that day. David assured my father they were ceremonially clean and had been for several days.

David also asked my father if he had any weapons on site. David said he didn't have a sword or spear because of the urgent nature of his mission from King Saul. So, my father told David that the sword of Goliath, the Philistine giant David had killed earlier, was in the tabernacle. It was wrapped in a cloth and hidden behind the place where he kept the ephod. David said, "There is no sword like it. Give it to me." And he took it. Many of us see the irony in this, since David had killed Goliath with a simple stone and slingshot—and now needs his sword!

---

[1] As Jesus explained in Matthew 12:3–4 (cf. Luke 6:9).

Has David become a Philistine, or Goliath himself?[2] Certainly, while he is called "a man after God's own heart," he is a man of clay feet like the rest of us. Perhaps the horrific outcome of this story has something to do with David taking Goliath's sword. We will never know.

Anyhow, this is where the story takes a brutal turn. For whatever reason, the man I mentioned at the beginning of the story, Doeg the Edomite, was inside the tabernacle. He was the chief shepherd of King Saul, a position of power in our kingdom. In fact, he was *de facto* a spy. He was there for some kind of ceremonial purpose and was for some reason "detained by the LORD." This would prove to be deadly for my father, the other priests and the people of Nob.

As I have said, King Saul is on the hunt. At the time David came to the tabernacle at Nob, King Saul and his men were in Gibeah, a town just north of Nob. King Saul found out where David was and gathered his men around him and berated them. He lashed out and asked the men whether they think David would give them all the fields and vineyards they were supposed to get as warriors. Did they want to be reduced to commanders of hundreds, when they are commanders of thousands under him? King Saul then became really whiny and asked them if this was the reason they had all conspired against him (which they hadn't) or why no one had told him that Jonathan had made a treacherous covenant with David. He complained no one cared about him and no one told him his son had actually incited David to ambush him (which Jonathan hadn't done). Paranoia and tyranny have come together in a pathetic King Saul.

Now, back to Doeg. He went to King Saul and reported how he had seen David at the tabernacle in Nob. He reported how David had spoken with my father and my father had given him food and the sword of Goliath. So King Saul called my father to appear before him. My father did so, along with me and the rest of my family—eight-six of us. Then the interrogation began. King Saul asked my father why he had conspired against him and given David the food and sword. He also asked why he let David ask God for direction by using the Urim and Thummim and said David is now "lying in wait" for him.

My father defended David by reminding King Saul there was no one more loyal to him than David, and how David was actually the

---

[2] I recall Bob Chisholm asking this question when reflecting on this event at the conference we shared at Elim Lodge Christian Resort and Conference Centre, which I mentioned in the Introduction.

king's son-in-law (married to his daughter Michal). He reminded King Saul that David was captain of the king's bodyguard and was highly respected in the king's household. He also reminded King Saul that this was not the first time David had come to him and asked for a word from God through him. So, why would the king be upset about that? My father said to the king there was no reason to accuse him of anything. He made it clear he didn't have knowledge of anything that was going on between him and David (perhaps the reason why David had not told the truth when he came to the tabernacle at Nob).

Well, that wasn't good enough for King Saul! He turned to the guards at his side and commanded them to kill us all. He said that we had sided with David and that we knew David was fleeing from him and that we didn't tell him. But the guards knew better, or perhaps were afraid to kill the priests of the Lord, and they refused to kill us.

Now Doeg appears on the scene again. Since the guards had refused to kill us, the king turned to Doeg and ordered him to do it. We were unarmed and the slaughter began. All of us—all eighty-five—except me, died. I escaped and fled to David. But the king did not stop there. Every living creature, human and animal, was massacred in the village of Nob. It was horrific. It was brutal. It is something I will never forget. The horrific irony of the whole thing is that such a massacre was the very thing King Saul refused to do under God's command with the Canaanite tribe, the Amalakites. What he would not do to his enemies, he did to his own people. Further, it was that very refusal that brought about his demise as king.

When I reached David, I relayed everything that had happened. It upset him greatly. He said to me, "That day when I went to the tabernacle and Doeg was there I knew there would be a problem. I knew he would tell King Saul." Then, in his grief and rage, he said to me, "I am responsible for all this, for the death of your father and your family. So, stay with me. You don't need to be afraid of me. King Saul, who is looking to kill you, is looking to kill me too. You will be safe with me."

So I did. In fact, I was able to bring the ephod from the tabernacle and used its Urim and Thummim several times when we were looking for direction from God. I eventually became high priest during David's kingship. But I met my demise under his son, King Solomon, when I participated in a rebellion against him thinking that Adonijah, his older brother, should inherit the kingdom. I should have been executed then, but King Solomon was merciful to me, saying that because I had been a faithful priest to his father he would allow me to live. I spent the rest of my days in my home town Anathoth, another village just north of Jerusalem.

This is my story about Doeg the Edomite. It is a horrific story. It is a story that reveals the brutality of humanity and the destructive results of a king, King Saul, who disobeyed the Lord. It is the story of God's people who wanted a king like the other nations. It is the story of a man, Doeg the Edomite, who would stop at nothing to gain favour with whoever was in power. Yet, there is a moment of grace. In spite of David's clay feet, there is goodness in the story. A fugitive takes in another fugitive. We became partners on the lam. The anointed king of the future and the remaining priests of my family travelled through the wilderness experiencing desolation and desperation together. Isn't this so often God's way of doing things?

Song ♦ Psalm 52

For the director of music. A maskil *of David. When Doeg the Edomite had gone to Saul and told him: "David has gone to the house of Ahimelek."*

1 Why do you boast of evil, you mighty hero?
    Why do you boast all day long,
      you who are a disgrace in the eyes of God?
2 You who practice deceit,
    your tongue plots destruction;
      it is like a sharpened razor.
3 You love evil rather than good,
    falsehood rather than speaking the truth.
4 You love every harmful word,
    you deceitful tongue!

5 Surely God will bring you down to everlasting ruin:
    He will snatch you up and pluck you from your tent;
      he will uproot you from the land of the living.
6 The righteous will see and fear;
    they will laugh at you, saying,
7 "Here now is the man
    who did not make God his stronghold

> > but trusted in his great wealth
> > and grew strong by destroying others!"
>
> 8 But I am like an olive tree
> > flourishing in the house of God;
> > I trust in God's unfailing love
> > for ever and ever.
> 9 For what you have done I will always praise you
> > in the presence of your faithful people.
> > And I will hope in your name,
> > for your name is good.

Introductory notes

Psalm 52 is rooted in a story of betrayal, betrayal by Doeg the Edomite, the chief herdsman of Saul. It's a song of David, of vindication and rage against a personal enemy, and it became a song for the nation, individually and communally. As are all the psalms, it was the song of Jesus. I wonder if he quietly prayed these words in his dealings with Judas Iscariot? It was the song of the first-century church and beyond, in their times of persecution and betrayals. Now, it is *our* psalm and song when we feel the deep pain of betrayal and deceit.

1. This psalm edges up to what we call imprecations or curses in the psalms.

We saw a similar thing in chapter one. It perhaps doesn't quite get there like other psalms do (eg. Pss 69:22–28; 109:6–15; 137:9). This whole topic has created significant consternation in the church and is something we need to talk about. Appendix A in Volume 2 has my understanding of this matter, and so I refer the reader to that essay.

2. David gave the psalm to the director of music for public distribution and use.

Psalm 52 became part of the worshipping voice of the people of God in the tabernacle, temple, synagogue and first-century church. While all the psalms were part of this public voice, this note makes it explicit.

3. It is called a *maskil*.

This term occurs in the series of Psalms 52 to 55, and also in Psalms 42, 44, 45, 74, 78, 88, 89 and 142. We are not sure what the term means, but many interpreters think it comes from a Hebrew word that means teaching, instruction or wisdom. In fact, in 2 Chronicles 30:22 the chronicler talks about a group of Levites who are called *maskilim*, ones who "showed good understanding" of the service of the Lord.

4. Doeg the Edomite

We know very little about this man other than what we read in this story. He appears nowhere else in Scripture. The fact he is identified three times as an Edomite is noteworthy since the Edomites, the descendants of Esau, were sworn enemies of Israel (cf. the Book of Obadiah).[3] We know Saul was in active war against them (1 Sam 14:47). It would seem that Doeg was either a captive of King Saul or a traitor to his people. As the chief shepherd, he would be in charge of all the other shepherds who were looking after Saul's animals. This would have been a position of power in King Saul's kingdom. We don't know why he was "detained before the LORD" at Nob. It is interesting that the prophet Jeremiah claimed the same kind of detention (Jer 36:5).[4] Doeg was a bloodthirsty and dangerous man, and he is the focus of David's indictments in our psalm.

5. The psalm is identified as a lament psalm.

Psalm 52 follows the general pattern of typical lament psalms with the complaint or distress described (vv. 1–4), the psalmist's confidence or expression of trust (vv. 5–7) and the concluding testimony and vow to praise (vv. 8–9). Often a lament psalm has an *explicit* appeal to God for deliverance. That is not part of this psalm, and we know that the standard structure of a lament psalm is not a straightjacket into which all such psalms must fall. Some

---

[3] Occasionally the Edomites were Israel's subordinates and vassal allies (cf. 2 Kgs 3:1–27).

[4] We are not sure why Jeremiah was detained. He had spoken powerfully against the aberrant worship at the temple, so perhaps he was banned by the priests because of those unpopular messages (cf. Jer 7:1—8:3; 19:1–20:6; 26:1–24). Also, King Jehoiakim was out to arrest Jeremiah and Baruch for the scroll Jeremiah had dictated to Baruch, which they were in hiding from the king (Jer 36:19, 25).

think this is more a psalm of trust. Certainly the trust element is strong in the psalm.

Psalm 52 has much in common with Psalm 49. Both speak about the arrogance of the wicked and the reliance on wealth rather than God. Psalm 49 is a wisdom psalm, and there are echoes of wisdom in Psalm 52 as well. It specifically warns the young that trusting in wealth and engaging in violence is the way of death. To trust in these values is also to be subject to the laughter of the righteous. Further, wisdom literature is characterized by the contrast of the wicked and righteous. Psalm 52 follows that pattern by contrasting an uprooted tree (v. 5) and a flourishing olive tree (v. 8). So, the element of wisdom is also part of Psalm 52 and consistent with the psalm being a *maskil*, if, in fact, the term reflects the idea of wisdom or teaching.

6. The psalm is in a group of psalms attributed to David.

Not only is this psalm part of a small collection of *maskil* psalms (Pss 52–55), it is also the second of a section of fifteen psalms attributed to David (Pss 51–65). There are seventy-three psalms attributed to David throughout the Book of Psalms. So, we have what we might call a subcollection of Davidic psalms here.

It is interesting that this collection starts with the famous Psalm 51—a lament about his personal sin with Bathsheba. There is the strong sense that while David goes on the attack for his betrayal by Doeg, he does so as a failed and penitent sinner himself. This is similar to the great prophet Isaiah, who in Isaiah 5 pronounces six woes against the wickedness of Judah but saves the seventh woe for himself after seeing the vision "of the LORD Almighty" exalted on his throne in the heavenly temple (Isa 6:1–7).

These fifteen psalms are dominated by lament psalms. However, as we come to the final few, there are two psalms of trust (Pss 62; 63). The final psalm, Psalm 65, is a psalm of thanksgiving with a strong element of praise throughout the psalm. So, while lament is the dominant tenor of this collection of psalms, it ends with thanksgiving and praise. As a result, the structure of the collection reflects the general focus and movement of a lament psalm itself.

Outline of the psalm
Psalm 52 has four parts:

1. An opening challenge (v. 1)
2. An indictment of the wicked (vv. 2–4)
3. Confidence in God for vindication (vv. 5–7)
4. A concluding testimony and praise (vv. 8–9)

> **Message of the psalm**
> In Psalm 52 we see that the perpetrators of evil and violence against God's people are, and need to be, called out as part of the authentic worship of God. Ultimately, such people will be judged by God and the righteous will be vindicated and blessed by him. As a result, God's faithful people will praise him and hope in his good name.

Exposition

1. We challenge those who seek our destruction (v. 1).[5]

David addresses Doeg directly and challenges his boastfulness, destructiveness and pride. He calls him a *gibbor*, a "mighty hero." David had a whole band of men called *gibborim*, but Doeg was not one of them. As the chief shepherd in Saul's court, he evidently had immense power and influence. For him to be able to slaughter eighty-five priests and a whole village, there must have been others who were willing to follow his leadership and commands, even when Saul's guardsmen refused to obey their king.

The question, "Why do you boast?" reminds us of Jeremiah's great statement:

This is what the LORD says:

"Let not the wise boast of their wisdom
 or the strong boast of their strength
 or the rich boast of their riches,

---

[5] There is a textual issue in the second line of verse 1. The ESV has: "The steadfast love of God endures all the day" reflecting the Hebrew text. The Septuagint, the Greek translation of the Old Testament, amends the Hebrew to read "violence all the day," since for some to talk about the love of God in this verse seems contradictory to the flow of the verse. Both ideas make sense.

> but let the one who boasts boast about this:
>> that they have the understanding to know me,
> that I am the LORD, who exercises kindness,
>> justice and righteousness on earth,
>> for in these I delight,"
> declares the LORD (Jer 9:23–24).

As the people of God, our boast is not to be found in our intellect, knowledge, wisdom, education, power, strength, wealth or prosperity. Earlier Jeremiah said death had climbed into the windows of the people (Jer 9:21). Valuing these things above God is what death looks like.

Rather, our boast, our glory, is to be found in our relationship with God. In particular, it is found in loving what he loves, namely kindness or loyal love (*hesed*) to God and each other. It is in being people of justice (*mishpat*), which has everything to do with caring for the poor, widow and orphan and, more broadly caring for the marginalized and voiceless. It is in being people of righteousness (*tsedeqah*), which speaks of moral and ethical purity and uprightness. The apostle James captured similar points when he wrote,

> Religion that God our Father accepts as pure and faultless is this: to look after orphans and widows in their distress [justice] and to keep oneself from being polluted by the world [righteousness] (Jas 1:27).

As I noted previously, there is a textual issue with the opening verse in Psalm 52. Another way to translate this verse is:

> Why do you boast of evil, you mighty hero?
>> God's steadfast love is all day long.

In this reading of the text, right from the outset, David is affirming his confidence in God. Certainly such confidence comes later in the psalm (vv. 5–7), and so it is not out of place in the opening lines.

2. We indict the wicked for who they really are and what they are really like (vv. 2–4).

Now, in these verses, David describes the nature of this wicked man in strong and graphic terms such as: deceit, destruction, razor, evil, falsehood and harmful.

Twice David refers to the tongue (vv. 2, 4), which forms a bracketing word for these verses. In other words, the reference to the tongue begins and ends the indictment.

The tongue is often referred to in the psalms. Throughout the psalms, it is a major weapon used by the enemy and the wicked against the psalmist and God's people. Psalm 12 talks about the wicked use of the tongue as a source of lies, deceptive flattering speech, boasting and maligning. In contrast, the Lord's speech is flawless and like purified silver and refined gold (v. 6). James picks up this same theme and calls the tongue "a restless evil, full of deadly poison" (Jas 3:8).

While Doeg had the power to murder and massacre, it was what he reported to Saul that brought it on, and David indicts Doeg for that. David says Doeg's tongue was used to plot destruction. While a sword or spear could be sharpened to a razor sharp edge, it was the tongue that actually was the sharpened razor. Doeg's tongue was used to speak lies and deceit, presumably embellishing what he saw at the tabernacle with David and Ahimelech. Fundamentally, it was an expression of his love for evil rather than for good, as the psalm states. Further, David actually identifies Doeg with what he said. He actually defines him as a "deceitful tongue." Doeg had become what he had done.

It is a powerful point that David speaks of Doeg's tongue, rather than attacking his brutal actions. In fact, the psalm opens with a reference to Doeg's boasting—a use of the tongue. It helps us understand how what James wrote is really true. Our speech has immense potential for evil and destruction or for good. So, the call to *guard* our tongues (cf. Prov 21:23; 1 Pet 3:10) is to be heeded by all who seek to follow the way of Jesus.

As a note in passing, there is a *Selah* in middle of the stanza. Yes, we need to pause and reflect, even rise to our feet, as we hear these words.

3. We express our confidence that God will judge and vindicate (vv. 5–7).

David includes along with the "you" of Doeg, the "he" of his God for his confidence. This is where we bump up against an imprecation. Such expressions always call on God to act. It is never a response of personal vendetta or action, even though God may use human actions to accomplish his purposes.

In light of the fact that Doeg had slaughtered so many people, David addresses Doeg directly and promises him the same end. There is progression in the indictment: first, that he be brought down like the destruction of a building; then, that he be snatched and torn from his tent and rendered homeless; and finally, that he be uprooted from the land of the living, an expression of both exile and death.

It is interesting that David uses words of violent action in response to violent action. He uses words like "everlasting ruin," "snatch," "pluck," "uproot" and then a *Selah*—stop and think about this! This is not outside the way of Jesus or the way God will ultimately set the world right. The apostle John tells us in his Revelation that Jesus will come riding a white stallion with a sword coming out of his mouth, symbolizing violent action and words of justice. There will be blood running as high as the horses' bridles (Rev 19:11–21). So we dare not succumb to the pressure of thinking only about "gentle Jesus, meek and mild." On his robe and thigh will be inscribed, "KING OF KINGS AND LORD OF LORDS" (Rev 19:16). There is a day of judgement coming for all the Doegs of this world. This brings confidence for the people of God, and a warning for all who would dare stand and oppose God's kingdom. Now, we don't know how Doeg's life ended. We don't know if he died prematurely in some kind of literal fulfilment of this psalmic promise. But the warning is here, and such a sinister announcement should make all but the most cynical stop and think about what they are doing

Further, David, in a way, piles it on. He tells us that the righteous—the covenant people of God—will see and fear. There is a little play on words here. They will *see* (*yire'u*) and they will *fear* (*yira'u*). We hear the rhyming sound between these two verses. As the ultimate humiliation, they will laugh at Doeg, because he thought he was stronger than God, he trusted in his wealth and he thought he could grow strong by violence.

Is it right for a follower of Christ to laugh at the wicked for their vanity and sense of self-sufficiency? Well, God does! The psalmist writes:

> The One enthroned in heaven laughs;
> the Lord scoffs at them (Ps 2:4).

> But the Lord laughs at the wicked,
> for he knows their day is coming (Ps 37:13).

> But you laugh at them, LORD;
> you scoff at all those nations (Ps 59:8).

The laughter of God is addressed toward those who refuse to submit to the rule of the LORD. So, there is an edge to God's rule. The righteous not only see the rule and power of God, but in their worship of God they have a healthy fear of that rule and power. I would suggest that perhaps the divine prerogative becomes the human permission to do the same.

It is interesting that David points to Doeg's wealth as a source of his trust. We are not sure what this means. Perhaps Saul rewarded him handsomely for his actions. Perhaps this is a reference to the fact that he was the chief shepherd for Saul, a position of power with the benefit of being well paid. Wealth and power often go together and this can give people greater capacity to do wrong.

At the end of the stanza, David moves Doeg from a *gibbor*, a warrior, to a *gever*, a mere man. No Hebrew reader would miss the biting irony of this shift in words.

4. We testify to our resilience and decision to trust and praise God (vv. 8–9).

David concludes the psalm on a note of praise, characteristic of so many of the lament psalms. He has talked directly to Doeg as "you," about God as "he" and now moves to a series of "I" statements celebrating the sustaining grace and goodness of his God in his life. It is one of the most magnificent statements of praise we have anywhere in the Book of Psalms.

In contrast to being rooted out of the land of the living (Doeg), David is like a well-rooted olive tree—a tree that lives for hundreds of years and is well known for its longevity (cf. Jer 11:16; Hos 14:6). He is flourishing, and not just flourishing, but flourishing in the house of God. There were olive trees in Solomon's temple which symbolized the beauty that was part of the worship of the

LORD. It is important to remember it was in the sanctuary at Nob that David got into trouble in the first place. But now that he has been vindicated, that tabernacle, that sanctuary, was a place of prosperity, blessing and longevity. It was the place where he would come to endlessly trust God's unfailing love (cf. Ps 23:6).

David ends in doxology, and he specifically calls on the name of God as the source of his trust. There are multiple references to the name of God throughout the psalms. The name of God, *Yahweh*, was revealed to Moses at the burning bush. It announces the uniqueness and self-existence of the Israelite God. For David to say he has hope in the *name* of God is to say he has hope in God *himself* and in the Israelite God *alone*. David then says that name is *good*. He brings both God's goodness and his unfailing love into his doxology, echoing the closing words of the most famous psalm:

> Surely your goodness and love will follow me
>   all the days of my life,
> and I will dwell in the house of the LORD
>   forever (Ps 23:6).

Reflections and lessons

1. What do we learn about God?

(a) *God welcomes us to crash the gates of heaven with our hearts bared and our voices of lament loud and clear.* While the psalm is addressed to David's enemy, it is addressed to him in the presence of God and the people of God. God is not put off when we express our feelings of betrayal and our desire for vindication.

(b) We also learn *God will bring justice to the world and the wicked*. He will set the world right, and he does not ignore or turn a deaf ear to the cries of the oppressed and betrayed.

(c) Then, through David and Abiathar, we learn *the path God takes us on toward leadership and appropriate positions and power often leads through wilderness, humility, suffering and deep loss.* While this can be a hard journey, this is the way of Jesus as he brings redemption to the world.

2. What do we learn about ourselves as the people of God?

As followers of Jesus, we can expect betrayal as part of the journey. Jesus sang this psalm in the synagogue. Jesus was betrayed. Did he quietly sing it specifically of Judas? We don't know. But it was part of his voice of spirituality and worship. So, this story and psalm tell us about the way of Jesus, the final David.

With God, we can laugh at the ways of the world! The prophets laughed at the false gods and their makers (Jer 10:1–13), wisdom teachers laughed at foolishness (Prov 1:20–27) and the psalmists give us a voice to laugh at the ways of the world. Perhaps this is startling to us. But it is similar to the words of apostle Paul, who uses biting sarcasm to confront the divided Corinthian church when he wrote, "No doubt there have to be differences among you to show which of you have God's approval" (1 Cor 11:19). Jesus was not above a well-placed barb when he called the Pharisees blind guides leading the blind (Matt 15:14) or those who strain at a gnat but swallow a camel (Matt 23:24). He then turns the temperature up when he calls them a "brood of vipers" destined for hell (Matt 23:33). We know the words,

> The One enthroned in heaven laughs,
>   the Lord scoffs at them (Ps 2:4).

This is part of the way of Jesus.

The desire for wealth and power will take us down the path of death. All too often, deceit, betrayal and violence are part of the way many use to get there. Whether inside or outside the church, the aspiration for position, power, wealth and control all too often takes over our lives. Loyal love to God and each other, care and compassionate action for the weak and powerless and moral and ethical righteousness are abandoned. Psalm 52 is a subtle warning to those who pursue coveteousness and who may consciously or subconsciously think they can gain by deceit. When that happens, death has climbed into the windows of our lives, communities, workplaces, schools and churches.

We recognize that when we are the targets of the Doegs and Sauls of this world, we are in good company (David, Abimelech, and yes, Jesus). We respond by lamenting, yes, but faithfully trusting God to work out his will and ways, and we lament in community so that we can get help and affirmation from our fellow pilgrims.

3. What do we learn about the world?

The world is the place of Doeg. It is the place of betrayal, lying, destruction and death.

It is the world of Saul. No, not everyone is brutally evil in the world. Saul's men understood that the actions he called for were despicable and so they refused to act. But the world is a place where Doegs are harboured and affirmed. To betray and deceive in order to gain place and power is to be part of the world of Saul and Doeg. It is no place for the follower of Christ.

The world, however, is the place where God's people live out their faith. We are called to resilience, obedience, holiness, grace and love in that world. We are also called to speak out against injustice and unrighteousness, and even—at times—follow our God and Messiah with a touch of mockery in our voices.

The *gibbor* has become a *gever*. The uprooted tree has been replaced by a well-rooted tree. This laughter is double-edged. There is a taunting side to it, as we watch "how the mighty have fallen," but there is relief and joy as we realize that fate will pass us by if we remain faithful to God. The reward that awaits is compared to a flourishing olive tree in the temple of God.

Final word

In Psalm 52, David speaks of praising God "in the presence of your faithful people." Both lament and praise are *communal* actions. Although we certainly engage with God in these and many other ways on a *personal* level, the life of faith was never intended to be lived in isolation. There is always to be a communal reality to the life of faith. That communal reality not only includes praise and thanksgiving, which we tend to do well, but also lament and even imprecation. Sadly, we tend not to do communal lament very well. Ella Wheeler Wilcox's poem "Solitude" captures that tragedy:

Laugh, and the world laughs with you;
Weep, and you weep alone;
For the sad old earth must borrow its mirth,
But has trouble enough of its own.

Sing, and the hills will answer;
Sigh, it is lost on the air;
The echoes bound to a joyful sound,
But shrink from voicing care.

Rejoice, and men will seek you;
Grieve, and they turn and go;
They want full measure of all your pleasure,
But they do not need your woe.

Be glad, and your friends are many;
Be sad, and you lose them all,—
There are none to decline your nectared wine,
But alone you must drink life's gall.

Feast, and your halls are crowded;
Fast, and the world goes by.
Succeed and give, and it helps you live,
But no man can help you die.

There is room in the halls of pleasure
For a large and lordly train,
But one by one we must all file on
Through the narrow aisles of pain.[6]

Grieving alone is too often the reality in the church. We are uncomfortable with tears, and sometimes our theology of God's goodness moves in too quickly. Yes, David will praise in the presence of God's saints. But this psalm shows it takes time to get to that praise. Lament and imprecation are a critical part of that

---

[6] "Solitude" in Ella Wheeler Wilcox, *Poems of Passion* (Chicago: Belford Clarke, 1883), 131–132. It was originally published in the *New York Sun* in 1883. You can also find it online at https://www.poetrynook.com/poet/ella-wheeler-wilcox.

voice, and in one sense, lament and imprecation are also praise set in the minor key. Both need to be sung, prayed and lived out in the worshipping community.

CHAPTER 4

GOD IS MY HELP

BIBLE READING
1 Samuel 23:1–29
Psalm 54

Story ♦ 1 Samuel 23:1–29[1]

"Is not David hiding among us?" Words of betrayal. Words that prompted a song, a song found the Book of Psalms, Psalm 54. I am the court historian in King David's kingdom. Let me tell you the story of deceit and deliverance that prompted these words and this song.

David, the son of Jesse, has been anointed as the next king in Israel. But he is on the run, hiding in caves, foreign villages, desert

---

[1] There are two stories that involve the Ziphites going to Saul and asking whether or not he knows that David is hiding among them. The first story is found in 1 Samuel 23, and verse 19 has the exact words found in the title of Psalm 54. The second story, found in 1 Samuel 26, has the opening words, "Is not David hiding?" and then gives a more detailed description of where he is hiding in Ziphite territory.

The question is whether these are two separate incidents or the same incident with different scenes articulated. It does not seem appropriate to conflate the stories since fortresses, wherever he can find refuge. He has gathered about 600 men around him, *gibborim*—mighty men, warriors.

King Saul, irrational and possessed by an evil spirit, is relentlessly on the hunt for David. King Saul, the people's choice, found out about David's anointing and is furious. In his mind, his son Jonathan was the rightful heir to the throne. But King Saul and his family have been removed by God because of his flagrant failures in faith and obedience. He knew all this, and that has just made him more determined to kill his God-ordained successor. To add to his fury, his son Jonathan has become a sworn friend and ally of David. He has pledged his support to David by saying, "The LORD is witness between you and me, and between your descendants and my descendants forever." King Saul knows his family dynasty will never happen, and that reality just fuels his fury.

So David, "king-elect," and his men are on the run. At the same time, David knows the Israelite people are his people and will be the people of his kingdom. So, when he hears that Keilah, one of the villages on the edge of Judah, is being attacked and looted by the Philistines, their hostile neighbours on the coast to the west, his heart turns toward the town. Appropriately, he inquires of God what he should do. The terse answer, "Go, attack the Philistines and save Keilah."

But David's men are not happy with this answer or David's plan. They remind him they are not even safe in Judah where they are now. Going on the attack against the Philistines would make them more vulnerable. So David, a man of prayer, asks the LORD again. The terse answer comes back, "Go down to Keilah, for I am going to give the Philistines into your hand." This was enough. David and his men then head south and west. They counterattack the invading Philistines and save Keilah.

However, as his men had predicted, this exposes David to King Saul. King Saul sees his chance. He essentially says to his followers,

---

the biblical narrator does not. Further, the events and endings of each are very different. Also, the stories are separated by two significant events: first, David spares Saul's life in the cave (1 Sam 24:1–22), and second, in a story of great intrigue, David marries Abigail after her husband Nabal dies (1 Sam 25:1–44).

Most commentators link Psalm 54 to 1 Samuel 23, since the story fits with the passion and pathos of the psalm more congruently, and the title of the psalm is taken directly from this story. Hence, for the purposes of this chapter, I am going to use the 1 Samuel 23 text as the basis for the story and read the song in Psalm 54 from this story.

"Ah, ha! David has made a mistake. God has given him into my hands. He has locked himself inside a town with gates and bars. We can trap him there. Let's go!" King Saul's reference to God makes us all smile. King Saul has no reverence or relationship to God. He has long since abandoned God, and God has long since abandoned him. God is answering David's prayers as his anointed. He is silent with King Saul.

David heard of the impending attack by King Saul and called in Abiathar, the priest who had escaped King Saul's massacre in Nob and who had joined him at Keilah. Abiathar had brought with him the sacred coat called an ephod. The ephod contained the Urim and Thummim, stones or dice-like objects used to obtain messages from God. David, again a man of prayer, asks God whether or not the people of Keilah would betray him and hand him over to King Saul in order to protect themselves from the ravages of his attack. The answer returns, "They will." The citizens of Keilah knew of the massacre ordered by King Saul up in Nob and they did not want the same fate.

David is the anointed of God. He has both the prophet Gad and the priest Abiathar among his men, giving God's counsel and direction. King Saul, whose name means "to inquire" or "to seek," is the seeker of David, but he never seeks or inquires of God. David, the sought one, is regularly seeking God's wisdom and word. King Saul, rejected by God and now dominated by an evil spirit sent by God, has only himself and his own twisted mind (along with the occult; i.e., the witch of Endor) to decide where, when and how to exercise his rule and protect his throne. David *will* come to the throne. He will come as a seeker of God. But the path to the palace will wind through being sought in desert and cave, and in betrayal and deceit.

So, David and his men go on the run again. Further south they go into a region called the desert of Ziph, moving from cave to cave, fortress to fortress. Finally, they come to a place called Horesh in Ziph where they are able to settle in for a short time in spite of King Saul's relentless searching. The Ziphites were a family of the tribe of Judah, David's tribe, and so they thought they would be safe among their clanspeople.

While here, a wonderful moment of redemption and hope happens for David. Jonathan, his sworn friend and ally, at the risk of his own life, searches out David and finds him in Horesh. Jonathan is a man of God, a man of deep faith, grace and humility. In the face of David's deep discouragement and despair, Jonathan helps him find strength in God. This is what he says, "Don't be afraid. My father will not lay a hand on you. You will be king over Israel, and I will be second to you. Even my father Saul knows this." With this amazing blessing and promise, David and Jonathan make a covenant with each other. Jonathan then returns to his home in Gibeah, perhaps never to see David again. This was not the first time David and Jonathan had bonded in friendship with a covenant. Shortly after David's amazing defeat of Goliath, Jonathan had given David his princely robes as well as his sword, bow and belt. In doing so, he declared he would never seek the throne and would be loyal to his friend David whom God had anointed as king. However, Jonathan would never be that second person in David's kingdom. He would be killed, along with his father, in a battle with the Philistines on Mount Gilboa in northern Israel. But David would take in Jonathan's crippled son Mephibosheth and would care for him in his court.

David's time of safety and security in Horesh among the Ziphites is short-lived. Seeing a wonderful opportunity to get into the good books of King Saul, the Ziphites send a contingent of their people north to Saul at his home in Gibeah with this message, "Is not David hiding among us in the strongholds at Horesh, on the hill of Hakilah, south of Jeshimon? Now, Your Majesty, come down whenever it pleases you to do so, and we will be responsible for giving him into your hands."

"Is not David hiding among us?" These are words of betrayal, betrayal by David's own people. Words that prompted a song—a song of deep poignancy and beauty. As I said at the beginning, the song is found in Psalm 54, and the opening lines go like this:

> Save me, O God, by your name;
>   vindicate me by your might.
> Hear my prayer, O God;
>   listen to the words of my mouth.
> Arrogant foes are attacking me;
>   ruthless people are trying to kill me—
>   people without regard for God (vv. 1–3).

But at the centre of the psalm, the pivot point upon which the psalm turns, David writes:

God is my help

> Surely God is my help;
> the Lord is the one who sustains me (v. 4).

In a turn of hypocritical piety, King Saul blesses the Ziphites in the name of the Lord! This is certainly nothing but a cold and rote ritual blessing. He then instructs the Ziphites to spy and discover all the information they can of David's movements and whereabouts. "But watch out," he says, "I am told he is very crafty." The word *crafty* is the word used to describe the serpent in the garden of Eden. *Was King Saul now that serpent?* Then he promises them he will not stop at anything to search David out and kill him.

So, David and his men are on the run again. Ruthless men are on the hunt. *When will it end? When will the promises of God come true? When will that moment of anointing by Samuel bring David to the throne? When will the desert caves stop being his and his men's home?*

Off into the wilds of the desert they go again. They travel further south into the Desert of Maon, to "the rock," with King Saul and his troops hot on their heels. But this time it looks like it is over. King Saul has him trapped. David and his men are fleeing for their lives on one side of a mountain; King Saul and his men are closing in on him in a pincher movement from the other side. There is no place to go. It is going to be a bloody battle, and one that David was sure to lose, and die.

But the end was not yet. In amazement, David and his men watch King Saul's army stop and turn around. For some unknown reason, they cease their pincher movement, return to camp and then head west and north toward Philistine territory. What is this? What is happening? David and his men find out later that at the very point of victory over David, at the very apex of capturing and killing the quarry King Saul hated so vehemently, a messenger had come running to him with the unsettling announcement that the Philistines were attacking Israelite villages to the north and west. In the nick of time, King Saul breaks off his pursuit of David and goes to deal with the Philistine invasion. David and his men are saved from a sure massacre.

This is part of the story of God's providence and protection that brings King David to the throne where I now serve as his court historian. The people of Keilah would have given him up and the Ziphites saw their advantage in serving as King Saul's spies. But God, in his providential care and promises to David, uses a well-timed Philistine diversion, those same Philistines David had helped the town of Keilah defeat, to rescue him from the ruthless hands of King Saul. Surely David, at that moment, knew God's promises were sure, and God was the ultimate *gibbor* who would bring him to the throne.

One final note: that rock? They named it *Sela Hammahlekoth*, which came to mean "rock of parting"—the place where David and King Saul "parted." However, the name has a second meaning, "the smooth rock." Why is this important? This is the same term used to describe the five "smooth" stones David picked up in the brook of Valley of Elah the day he killed the Philistine giant Goliath. David is destined for the throne, and neither the Philistines nor King Saul could stop the powerful work of God, who was creating his nation and kingdom under his anointed shepherd king, David.

Song ♦ Psalm 54

For the director of music. With stringed instruments. A maskil *of David. When the Ziphites had gone to Saul and said, "Is not David hiding among us?"*

1. Save me, O God, by your name;
    vindicate me by your might.
2. Hear my prayer, O God;
    listen to the words of my mouth.

3. Arrogant foes are attacking me;
    ruthless people are trying to kill me—
    people without regard for God.

4. Surely God is my help;
    the Lord is the one who sustains me.

5. Let evil recoil on those who slander me;
    in your faithfulness destroy them.

6. I will sacrifice a freewill offering to you;
    I will praise your name, LORD, for it is good.
7. You have delivered me from all my troubles,
    and my eyes have looked in triumph on my foes.

Introductory notes
This psalm arises out of one of David's greatest testing experiences. The contrasts of hope found in the visit by Jonathan, the desperate disappointment because of the betrayal by his own tribal family, the fatigue because of the relentless pursuit of Saul, the despair of that looming defeat on the mountain in the Desert of Maon and the joy of that unexpected providential turn of events orchestrated by God using the Philistines, the enemies of David, pour out into the words of this psalm.

1. This psalm is addressed to the director of music.
As a lament psalm, the voice of lament was a powerful way of expressing worship to God. Authentic worship emerges from everyday realities. It is not something only expressed in isolated environments, such as a Sunday morning worship service where worshippers are often encouraged to set aside the cares and troubles of the week and focus attention on God. Worship in the Book of Psalms never displays that dichotomy.

2. The psalm was to be played with stringed instruments.
The psalm was to be sung using a harp or other stringed instrument. The phrase is found in seven psalms: Psalms 4, 6, 54, 55, 61, 67 and 76. Psalm 5 has the phrase "for wind instruments." This refers to some kind of horn or flute. This is not to say that these are the only psalms that used stringed or wind instruments. Such instruments were widely used in the singing and praises of Israel (cf. 2 Chron 7:6; 29:25–27; Pss 98:5–6; 150:3–5). However, these psalms in particular are identified to be accompanied by these specific musical instruments.

3. The psalm is called *maskil* of David.
We've seen the term *maskil* before in Psalm 52. It is evidently a musical term, perhaps rooted in a word meaning *instruction* or *wisdom*.

Outline of the psalm
Psalm 54 follows the classic lament psalm structure. These kinds of psalms are found throughout the ancient near east and inevitably wrap around a standard form:

1. An address to God
2. A complaint or statement of distress
3. A cry for help
4. A confession of trust
5. A concluding vow to praise

Not all lament psalms follow this exact pattern or have all the elements of the form. But the structure guided the poets as they created their poems and songs.

Psalm 54 is divided into these traditional five parts:

1. The cry for help to God (address to God) (vv. 1–2)
2. The complaint (v. 3)
3. The confession of trust (v. 4)
4. A call for God to judge (an expression of trust) (v. 5)
5. The vow to praise (vv. 6–7)

Further, the psalm pivots on verse 4 with David's faith statement, "Surely God is my help; the Lord is the one who sustains me," standing at the apex of the psalm.

> **Message of the psalm**
> In Psalm 54 we find a prayer for deliverance from ruthless attackers and confidence in God for deliverance and triumph. In such dangerous and desperate times, we hear the voice of worship that includes the full reality of the pain being endured and the call on God to invade. In faith, we praise God for our deliverance and triumph.

Exposition

1. We cry out to God for salvation and vindication (vv. 1–2).

Diverging somewhat from the classic lament psalm in which the distress or complaint is usually expressed immediately following the address to God, David takes us straight into the cry for help. This increases the sense of urgency that this psalm embraces.

As we so often find in the psalms, David addresses his cry for help to God. He is a man of faith, even though he is bold in his prayers. Exposing our hearts and our deep feelings of desperation and hopelessness is not antithetical to faith. In fact, it is crucial to our faith. It creates an authenticity that cannot be expressed in any other way.

We observe that the call for saving is rooted in the *name* of God, an idea shared with Psalm 52 and David's encounter with Doeg the Edomite. It is interesting that this psalm, and most of the others we are considering, is found in Book Two of the Psalter, the Elohistic Psalter (Pss 42–72).[2] *Elohim* occurs 201 times in contrast to the name *Yahweh*, which only occurs forty-four times, and which tends to be the dominant name used throughout the rest of the Psalter.

As we noted in Psalm 52, the name being referred to is *Yahweh*, the personal name of God revealed to Moses at the burning bush (Exod 3:14–15). It is the name that excludes all other deities as contenders for supremacy, and was the name that stood behind the covenant God made with his people. David is calling on his *covenant God* to save him from his enemies. He is calling on God to be faithful to his covenant with him as anointed king and on the people he will rule. He identifies the name as *Yahweh* (the LORD) in verse 6 in his vow to praise.

However, the parallel line in verse 1 speaks of God's might or power. This brings in the name *Elohim*, which is used four times throughout the psalm. The name *Elohim* is rooted in the same name as the Canaanite god *El* who was a kind of grandfather of the Canaanite pantheon. The word means *strong* or *powerful* and the Hebrew writers expanded the word by adding a syllable *oh* in order to make the name more grandiose. Then the Hebrew writers put it in the plural form *im*. There has been much discussion of why *Elohim* is plural, and many think that this is a subtle way to communicate a triune God. This may be true, but it is well established that the Hebrews would make a word plural in order to elevate its importance. It is sometimes called a "plural of majesty." Since *im* has no specific reference to the quantity of three, I have tended to see the *im* on *Elohim* as this plural of majesty.

---

[2] See chapter 1, note 3.

This is consistent with the insertion of an additional syllable for basically the same purpose.

David is appealing to both his covenant God *and* his God of power and strength in the precarious place in which he finds himself. He needs God's faithfulness to him as his covenant servant. He also needs a strong God, an *Elohim*, to invade and protect him against the Ziphites and the forces of Saul that were coming against him.

In these verses, he also calls on God to "vindicate" him. He has done no wrong. In fact, he has risked his and his men's lives by taking on the Philistines at Keilah and has exposed his whereabouts to Saul in doing so. David is frustrated in that, by doing what is right and good, he is now being betrayed. The call to be and do right and good is not a guaranteed path to a blessed and prosperous life. The life of faith is a journey with God through difficult and painful realities. The end is guaranteed in the promises of a new heavens and earth, but the life of faith is lived in the now, in a beautiful but broken world with hostile people with names and places that are real. But it is a world that has the fresh strength, new mercies and presence of God every morning (cf. Lam 3:23). The psalm opens with a passionate address to God. It is an act of worship. It teaches us how to pray.

2. We complain to God about the brutality we are facing (v. 3).
In the climax of the description of his enemies, David doesn't hold back from what he wants to say. Saul and the Ziphites are "arrogant foes" and "ruthless people." They will stop at nothing to hunt him down and see him dead. Whether it was the townspeople of Keilah who were prepared to give him up to avoid the wrath of Saul, whether it was the Ziphites, David's own tribal clanspeople, who were looking for favour and advantage with Saul or whether it was Saul and his men, "ruthless" was the best possible term he could use.

But then a third line is added, and the intensity increases even more. In the same vein as Psalms 52 and 53, they are described as "people without regard for God." Israel was a theocratic state. It was a monarchy ruled by a human king. But the ultimate king was their God, the Lord himself. To declare that those who were to betray or destroy him had no regard for God, indicated they had completely lost their moorings as a people of God. Further, their king, Saul, had abandoned his sacred trust to rule the nation as a king under the authority of God.

The intensity of the circumstances for David was almost beyond imagination. In David's voice, we find our own. No, we are not being chased by a demented king or being betrayed by Ziphites. But we find ourselves in our own worlds of desperation, pain, brutality and ruthlessness. This prayer did not stay with David. It became the voice of the nation, the voice of Jesus, the voice of the first-century church and now it is ours. It is harsh and real. So, it is not a surprise that we have a *Selah* at the end of verse 3. We need to pause, perhaps stand or kneel and reflect deeply on the depth and seriousness this prayer brings to our life of prayer and piety.

3. We centre our thoughts with a confession of trust (v. 4).

We come now to the pivot or hinge verse of the psalm. Everything is perfectly balanced on this verse. The Hebrew poets often used a central verse or line to create the primary thought of their poems. A classic example of this is the rhetorical question in Psalm 113:5 where right in the centre of this beautiful psalm of praise the psalmist asks, "Who is like the LORD our God, the One who sits enthroned on high?" While Psalm 113 follows the classic form of a praise psalm: (1) call to praise (vv. 1–3); (2) reasons for praise (vv. 6–9a); (3) conclusion to praise (v. 9b), complete with the framing statement, "Praise the LORD," the psalm pivots on that question with the obvious answer, "No one." We could cite numerous other examples of this kind of literary pivot point (eg. Pss 1:3b; 8:4; 21:7; 42:8 [with Ps 43]; 67:4; 97:7).

With a reference to God—the God of ultimate strength and power—he affirms his God's help. God has resources and abilities beyond what he had. He is a man of dependence, not autonomy or self-sufficiency. To go on his own resources would only lead to death. It was the providential arrival of the messenger with the message the Philistines were invading that saved the day for David. Left to his own resources, it would have been a fight to the death.

David doubles down on the name *God* in the next line with the name *Lord*, *Adonai*. This is the name used for a master, lord or king. It speaks of *power*, but also of *position*. It overlaps with *Elohim*, and adds the notion of God as his *master*, not just his mighty *helper*. Often the one who is able to help holds a higher position in the relationship or has more resources than the one receiving help. It is a reminder that the ones with power and position are the ones most often able to help. This relationship stands behind the word *justice*, used so often by the prophets. For the prophets, it is both a king and a nation who are committed to justice that are blessed by God. The word has everything to do with the powerful caring for the poor, orphan and widow—the ones with *no* power (cf. Isa 1:17). The first duty of those who have been given the privilege and responsibility of leadership and power is to ensure that the powerless are cared for. This is the foundation for basic civility in a nation, community, family or church (cf. Jas 1:27).

The central message that David brings out in his song is that God, his Lord (*Adonai*), is the one who helps and sustains him. As his people took up the song, and as Jesus sang it in the synagogue, the first-century church sang it as part of their worship. Further, the church has sung this song for centuries, and we sing it in our time. We sing of the fact that our anchored trust and confidence in our God to help and sustain, remains the bedrock of our faith.

4. We call on God to judge those who oppose us (v. 5).

As is characteristic of David and all the psalmists, they are not shy to call on God to act in judgement and vindication. Edging up to *imprecation*, David calls on God to repay the evil planned for him on those who are attacking and slandering him.[3] He is not asking God to let him wreak his own vengeance and wrath, rather he is handing it over to his God to act on his behalf.

Further, he roots it in God's faithfulness, his *'emet*. The Hebrew word means *truth*. But it goes beyond the notion of objective truth or veracity, into the idea of trust, truthfulness, faithfulness, even endurance. It is often linked with the word *hesed*, which speaks of God's covenant loyalty to his people (cf. Exod 34:6; Prov 3:3). God is not only the repository of truth but also the one that can be depended on over the long haul.

God has made a covenant with his people. He made it in stages through Abraham, Moses and David in old covenant times, and he

---

[3] See Appendix A in Volume 2 for my essay on the use of imprecations in the church today.

has brought it to culmination through Christ in the New Testament and into our times as the church.[4] He has promised to be faithful to his people, and David invokes that promise. God's faithfulness is often experienced in the most dire of times. God does not *remove* his people from the brokenness and brutality of a fallen creation, rather he journeys with them through those times, often times of deep loss and grief. One of the most shattering of times for the people of God was the destruction of Jerusalem and the exile of Judah by the Babylonians. Psalm 137 catches the deep pain of that experience, "By the rivers of Babylon we sat down and wept" (v. 1).

The entire Book of Lamentations does so as well. Poem after poem, four of them written as alphabetic acrostics seeking to communicate the totality of the pain, cry out with the excruciating pain of that horrific event. But, almost surprisingly, almost shockingly, at the very centre of the book of Lamentations (another poetic apex or hinge as it were) we find these words:

> Because of the LORD's great love [*ḥesed*] we are not consumed,
>   for his compassions ["mother love"] never fail.
> They are new every morning;
>   great is your faithfulness [*'emet*] (Lam 3:22–23).

One of the most well-known hymns of the church builds on that statement, "Great Is Thy Faithfulness." As we sing that great hymn of the faith, we need to understand that the faithfulness we celebrate and sing about in that majestic hymn is not rooted in a life of ease or comfort or in God removing us from all that is hard and hurtful. It is rooted in disaster and catastrophe. These are the times when we cry out in deep despair on one hand as Lamentations does, but at the same time centring our hope and confidence on the faithfulness of God when it seems things can't get any worse.

5. We proclaim our vow to praise and worship (vv. 6–7).
In the typical way that a lament psalm ends, we hear David announce he will sacrifice a freewill offering because deliverance

---

[4] The best understanding of God's covenants with his people in the Old Testament and culminating in Christ and into the church is Peter J. Gentry and Stephen J. Wellum, *Kingdom Through Covenant: A Biblical-Theological Understanding of the Covenants* (Wheaton: Crossway, 2012).

has happened. The Hebrews had three categories of offerings: the propitiatory sacrifices of sin offerings and guilt offerings, the burnt offering as a personal or communal consecratory offerings and then several communal offerings to express peace with God and each other or for various occasions such as dedications, vows or simply as an act of worship. The offering David refers to here is in the third category. It is simply an expression of worship and gratitude for the goodness of God. The beauty of the sacrifice is that it was done publicly so family and friends could participate in the pain and joy of David's experience.

The offering is an expression of praise. This time it is to the name *Yahweh*, one of the rare instances of the occurrences of this name in Book Two of the Psalter. David reminds himself and his people that their God is the God that has made covenant with them. He reminds them that *Yahweh*, the LORD, is the God who simply *is*, and that he is *good*. The concluding testimony of David in Psalm 52:8–9 captures a similar theme wrapped around the name of God.

God's name is good. Asaph, one of the worship leaders when David came to the throne, sang about the goodness of God in his beautiful but difficult Psalm 73. He starts the song with "Surely God is good to Israel, to those who are pure in heart" (v. 1). But then for thirteen verses he plunges into all that is wrong in the world. He laments his seeming worthless efforts to stay faithful to God and be pure in life. But then he journeys back from the edge of abyss with the terse comment, "till I entered the sanctuary of God" (v. 17). Evidently the signs and symbols of the tabernacle brought him back to his spiritual senses, and he concludes at the end of the psalm not with "God is good" (that's been established in v. 1), but "it is good *to be near God*" (v. 28). He moves from an objective notion of the goodness found in God to the subjective reality of the goodness of a *relationship* with God. David is surely thinking similarly as he reflects on his covenant God *Yahweh*, whom he knows and worships from both an objective and subjective relationship. Someone said to me once, "God is good and all he does is goodness." There are many times, when the waters are deep and the night is dark, I am not sure of that statement. But David helps us see that truth through the eyes of faith. Yes, dimly at times, but David helps us know the experience of God's sustaining presence when life becomes almost impossible to bear.

The surprising part of the ending of Psalm 54 is that David speaks as if his troubles are now over. While he may be referring to his providential deliverance from Saul when that messenger arrived, it is hardly the end of David's troubles. His ultimate triumph over his enemies and his coronation as king are still a very distant hope. But, this is the language David uses. While he and his men were certainly grateful for the rescue of the moment, it seems David is looking far beyond that deliverance and triumph to a much greater one, perhaps even one that surpassed the promise of his messianic rule. He is stating his confidence that he has been heard and delivered, but he is not locking God into what final deliverance and triumph might look like. The confidence is in God *himself*, his will, his ways, his Word. In pointing himself to God, David leads the way for us.

Reflections and lessons

1. What do we learn about God?

(a) We learn through the names of God in Psalm 54 that *God is a God of might and power* (*Elohim*), he is master, lord and king (*Adonai*) *and he is the God of covenant faithfulness* and unique in the world as the one who simply *is* (*Yahweh*). All three of these names are captured in Jesus of Nazareth who is the *Word*, who reveals the full Godhead. We see Jesus in a new and fresh light.

(b) Further, *God is our help and helper* (*'ezer*). Often we think that a helper is inferior in status, some kind of servant. The reality is our God, who certainly is not inferior in any way, is the One we all need because of our lack of self-sufficiency. It is because of *his* status and power that he is able to bring needed help into our lives.

However, God comes to us as our servant, in humility and compassion, to provide sustaining grace in our time of need. Jesus is all about servanthood. God defines him as a servant (cf. Isa 42:1; 50:10; 52:13), Jesus himself made it clear the way of his kingdom is servanthood (Mark 10:43) and the apostle Paul pointed to the servanthood of Jesus as the path to exaltation and worship

(Phil 2:6–11). This helps us understand what God saw in Eve as he called her Adam's *'ezer*, in order to solve the "not good" status of Adam alone in the garden (Gen 2:18).

(c) But *God is also the One who brings about ultimate judgement and justice*. "'It is mine to avenge: I will repay,' says the Lord" (Rom 12:19). While imprecation is still a prayer for the church (cf. the apostle Paul's imprecation of anyone who would preach a false gospel, Gal 1:8–9), we learn from David that we are to give such a prayer over to God. In a world where we see so much cruelty and violence, sometimes it is hard to actually believe in this God. But by declaring our confidence in God in this way, we show we truly do believe God exists, is active in history and is a God of justice who will set the world to rights.

2. What do we learn about ourselves as the people of God?

We are invited to crash the gates of heaven in prayer, lament and imprecation. Such prayers are deep and authentic worship. We may have been taught to be docile and polite in prayer. But the psalms take us elsewhere, both in relation to God and in relation to the world arrayed against God and his kingdom. Yes, we are to love our enemies, but that does not stop us from raising our voices in protest to God in the name of justice, righteousness and loving-kindness (cf. Jer 9:23–24).

We learn God's faithfulness is all about living confidently in the here and now. His faithfulness during difficulty works itself out in familiar places, with familiar people and in familiar circumstances (remember, the Ziphites were a family clan in David's tribe of Judah). God's faithfulness is not an escape hatch from life. It's something that journeys *with us* in times of loss and joy, and often through people close to us.

Like David, we can draw the conclusion of final vindication and salvation now. It is a *present* reality celebrated in the hope of the *ultimate* reality. Salvation has been accomplished through Christ—birth, life, death, resurrection, ascension, rule. Yes, it is "not yet." But we live in the confidence of God's help in the now, in the sure reality of the "not yet."

3. What do we learn about the world?

The world can be ruthless against God's people. It is interesting that David and his men initially found haven among their own clanspeople. However, it didn't last. Perhaps it was the the fear of what happened at Nob or the opportunity for advantage in betrayal that proved too much for the Ziphites to sustain sheltering David. Even when the world does good for God's people, the fear or pressures of retribution from a system arrayed against God and his kingdom will often push back against the mission and message of the gospel that God's people embrace and proclaim. Civil and societal good done as the church in Christ's name is often embraced in the immediate. But eventually the resentment and fear of what the church actually is will turn the world against it. Or it will put huge pressure on the church to soften the message of redemption that comes with bringing good to the world.

Many excellent Christian service organizations have resisted this pressure. But often there is minimal help coming from societal and government resources to ensure these social justice and service organizations flourish.[5]

There are many powers arrayed to thwart the justice of God's kingdom. But the world will be subject to the victory of God. God and his kingdom are destined for triumph.

> That at the name of Jesus every knee should bow,
>   in heaven and on earth and under the earth,
> and every tongue acknowledge that Jesus Christ is Lord,
>   to the glory of God the Father (Phil 2:10–11).

Final word

While Thomas O. Chisholm's classic hymn "Great Is Thy Faithfulness" is rooted in Lamentations 3:22–23, it forms a fitting final thought to our reflections as we focus on Psalm 54:3, the pivot point of the psalm.

> Great is Thy faithfulness, O God my Father;
> There is no shadow of turning with Thee;

---

[5] I have firsthand knowledge of this reality through my involvement in a Christian social justice organization in the city where I live.

Thou changest not, Thy compassions, they fail not;
As Thou hast been, Thou forever will be.

> *Refrain*
> Great is Thy faithfulness!
> Great is Thy faithfulness!
> Morning by morning new mercies I see.
> All I have needed Thy hand hath provided;
> Great is Thy faithfulness, Lord, unto me!

Summer and winter and springtime and harvest,
Sun, moon and stars in their courses above
Join with all nature in manifold witness
To Thy great faithfulness, mercy and love.
> *Refrain*

Pardon for sin and a peace that endureth,
Thine own dear presence to cheer and to guide;
Strength for today and bright hope for tomorrow,
Blessings all mine, with ten thousand beside![6]
> *Refrain*

---

[6] Thomas O. Chisholm, "Great Is Thy Faithfulness," Public Domain, 1923.

SELECTED BIBLIOGRAPHY

Anderson, Bernhard W., with Stephen Bishop. *Out of the Depths: The Psalms Speak for Us Today*. 3rd ed. Revised and expanded. Philadelphia: Westminster John Knox, 2000.

Barker, David G. "The Church and Imprecations in the Psalms: The Place of the Call to Curse in the Life of the Church Today." In *Ecclesia Semper Reformanda Est—The Church is Always Reforming. A Festschrift on Ecclesiology in Honour of Stanley K. Fowler*. Eds. David G. Barker, Michael A.G. Haykin and Barry H. Howson. Kitchener: Joshua Press, 2016, 65–87.

Bellinger Jr., W.H. *Psalms as a Grammar For Faith: Prayer and Praise*. Waco: Baylor University Press, 2019.

Bergen, Robert D. *1–2 Samuel*. NAC. Nashville: Broadman and Holman, 1996.

Beyerlin, Walter, ed. *Near Eastern Religious Texts Relating to the Old Testament*. Trans. J. Bowden. London: S.C.M., 1978.

Billings, J. Todd. *Rejoicing in Lament: Wrestling with Incurable Cancer & Life in Christ*. Grand Rapids: Brazos, 2015.

Boda, Mark J. *After God's Own Heart: The Gospel According to David*. Phillipsburg: P&R Publishing, 2007.

Brueggemann, Walter. *The Message of the Psalms: A Theological Commentary*. Minneapolis: Augsburg, 1984.

Carter, Craig A. "Just Another Angel? The Angel of the Lord and the Doctrine of the Trinity." In *Reading Scripture, Learning Wisdom: Essays in Honour of David G. Barker*. Ed. Michael A.G. Haykin and Barry H. Howson. Peterborough: Joshua Press, 2021, 61–75.

Chisholm Jr., Robert B. "A Theology of the Psalms." In *A Biblical Theology of the Old Testament*. Ed. Roy B. Zuck. Chicago: Moody, 1991, 257–301.

Cohen, David J. "'Why O Lord?' Lament as the Window of the Human Experience of Distress." In *Finding Lost Words: The Church's Right to Lament*. Eds. G. Geoffrey Harper and Kit Barker. Eugene: Wipf & Stock, 2017, 72

Day, John N. *Crying for Justice: What the Psalms Teach Us about Mercy and Vengeance in an Age of Terrorism*. Grand Rapids: Kregel, 2005.

deClaisse-Walford, Nancy, Rolf A. Jacobson and Beth LaNeel Tanner. *The Book of Psalms*. NICOT. Grand Rapids: Eerdmans, 2014.

Evans, Paul. *1–2 Samuel*. SGBC. Grand Rapids: Zondervan, 2018.

Gentry, Peter J. and Stephen J. Wellum. *Kingdom Through Covenant: A Biblical-Theological Understanding of the Covenants*. Wheaton: Crossway, 2012.

Gesenius' Hebrew Grammar. Ed. Emil Kautzsch; trans. Arthur E. Cowley. 2nd ed. Oxford: Clarendon, 1910.

Goldingay, John. *Psalms. Vol. 2: Psalms 42–89*. Baker Commentary on the Old Testament: Wisdom and Psalms. Grand Rapids: Baker Academic, 2007.

_____. *Walk On: Life, Loss, Trust, and Other Realities*. Grand Rapids: Baker Academic, 2002.

Greidanus, Sidney. *The Modern Preacher and the Ancient Text*. Grand Rapids: Eerdmans, 1988.

Hill, Andrew. *1 & 2 Chronicles*. NIVAC. Grand Rapids: Zondervan, 2010.

Jenkins, Steffen G. *Imprecations in the Psalms: Love for Enemies in Hard Places*. Eugene: Pickwick, 2022.

Johnson, Darrell W. *The Glory of Preaching: Participating in God's Transformation of the World*. Downers Grove: IVP Academic, 2009.

Kidner, Derek. *Psalms 1–72*. Tyndale Old Testament Commentaries. Downers Grove: InterVarsity, 1973.
Klein, William W., Craig L. Blomberg and Robert L. Hubbard. *Introduction to Biblical Interpretation*. 3rd ed. Grand Rapids: Zondervan, 2017.
Korkidakis, Jon. *Touching God: Discovering Prayer That Moves the Heart of God*. Eugene: Wipf & Stock 2021.
Leithart, Peter. *1 and 2 Chronicles*. BTCB. Grand Rapids: Brazos, 2019.
Lewis, C.S. *Prince Caspian: The Return to Narnia*. London: Fontana Lions, 1980.
_____. *Reflections on the Psalms*. London: Harcourt Brace Jovanovich, 1958.
Peterson, Eugene. *Answering God: The Psalms as Tools for Prayer*. New York: HarperCollins, 1989.
Roper, David. *A Burden Shared: An Encouragement for Those Who Lead*. Grand Rapids: Discovery House, 2016.
Ross, Allan P. *A Commentary on the Psalms*. Vol. 1. Grand Rapids: Kregel, 2011.
Taylor, W. David O. *Open and Unafraid: The Psalms as a Guide to Life*. Nashville: Thomas Nelson, 2020.
Thompson, Alan J. "'Consolation for the Despairing:' C.H. Spurgeon's Endorsement of Lament Psalms in Public Worship." In *Finding Lost Words: The Church's Right to Lament*. Eds. G. Geoffrey Harper and Kit Barker. Eugene: Wipf & Stock, 2017, 43–44.
Tsumura, David T. *The First Book of Samuel*. NICOT. Grand Rapids: Eerdmans, 2007.
_____. *The Second Book of Samuel*. NICOT. Grand Rapids: Eerdmans, 2019.
VanGemeren, Willem A. *Psalms*. EBC. Vol 5. Grand Rapids: Zondervan, 1991.
Villanueva, Federico G. *It's OK Not To Be OK: Preaching the Lament Psalms*. Carlisle: Langham Preaching Resources, 2017.
Waltke, Bruce K., James M. Houston and Erika Moore. *The Psalms as Christian Lament: A Historical Commentary*. Grand Rapids: Eerdmans, 2014.
_____. *The Psalms as Christian Worship: A Historical Commentary*. Grand Rapids: Eerdmans, 2010.

Weiser, Artur. *The Psalms: A Commentary*. Philadelphia: Westminster John Knox Press, 1962.

Wilson, Gerald H. *Psalms*. Vol. 1. NIVAC. Grand Rapids: Zondervan, 2002.

Wright, N.T. *The Case for the Psalms: Why They Are Essential*. New York: HarperOne, 2013.

Youngblood, Ronald F. *1 & 2 Samuel*. EBC. Grand Rapids: Zondervan, 1992.

Dominus Deus fortitudo mea | The sovereign LORD is my strength

www.ingramcontent.com/pod-product-compliance
Lightning Source LLC
Chambersburg PA
CBHW072100110526
44590CB00018B/3256